PRAISE FOR THE VAGABONDING WITH KIDS SERIES

"Refreshing, honest, and humorous. I couldn't put it down!"
—Vicky Etherington, *Eat Sleep Love Travel*

"A hilarious and uncensored adventure—Turner's stories of family travel go from cute as a koala bear to crazy as a Tasmanian devil faster than your kids can say, 'Are we there yet?'"
—Susanne Kerns, *The Dusty Parachute*

"Capturing the real face of family travel—the laughs, anxiety, and adjustments—*Vagabonding with Kids: Australia* takes you on the trip of a lifetime to the land Down Under. A brilliant read for all parents, travelers, and wanderlusters."
—Alyson Long, *World Travel Family*

". . . a rollicking, outrageous, hilarious adventure. Buckle up!"
—Michelle Newman, *You're My Favorite Today*

"Adventurous, funny, and inspirational, this book will convince you that traveling with kids isn't impossible. It's irresistible."
—Karen Alpert, *New York Times* bestselling author of *I Heart My Little A-Holes* and *I Want My Epidural Back*

"Everyone dreams of escaping the 9-to-5, but few have the guts to actually do it. AK dares to live her life on purpose and has realized early in life that true riches aren't reflected in accumulated possessions but are the vast and unique experiences we collect. If you're ready to dive into the digital nomad lifestyle, you must read this book. AK proves anyone can do it—even a family!"
—Christy Hovey, *The 9-to-5 Escape Artist: A Startup Guide for Aspiring Lifestyle Entrepreneurs and Digital Nomads*

ALSO BY AK TURNER

VAGABONDING WITH KIDS SERIES

Vagabonding with Kids
Vagabonding with Kids: Australia

TALES OF IMPERFECTION SERIES

This Little Piggy Went to the Liquor Store
Mommy Had a Little Flask
Hair of the Corn Dog

Vagabonding
with kids
BRAZIL

AK TURNER

BROWN BOOKS
PUBLISHING GROUP

Vagabonding with Kids: Brazil

Brown Books Publishing Group
16250 Knoll Trail Drive, Suite 205
Dallas, Texas 75248
www.BrownBooks.com
(972) 381-0009

A New Era in Publishing®

ISBN 978-1-61254-919-4
LCCN 2016949847

Printed in the United States
10 9 8 7 6 5 4 3 2 1

Design by Sarah Tregay, DesignWorks Creative, Inc.
Cover photos by Amaura Mitchell and iStock
Author photo by Mike Turner

For more information or to contact the author, please go to
VagabondingWithKids.com or AKTurner.com.

For my in-laws.
They've earned it.

RIO NEGRO

AMAZON RIVER

Manaus ○

AMAZON
RAIN FOREST

Brasília

Salvador ○
Itacaré ○
Ilhéus ○
Arraial d'Ajuda ○
Trancoso ○

Itaúnas ○

Guarapari ○

Porecatu ○
Londrina ○
Salto do
Apucaraninha ○

Rio de Janeiro ○ ○ Búzios
○ ○ Arraial do Cabo
○ São Paulo

N

ATLANTIC OCEAN

CONTENTS

Brazilian Blessings

*The greatest obstacle to international understanding
is the barrier of language.*

—Christopher Dawson

"*As crianças' mãos! As crianças' mãos!*"
I'd studied Portuguese for six months in preparation; I'd
been in Brazil for less than an hour. This was my first test. The
security guard had started with a more verbose reprimand,
but her frustration with my lack of understanding reduced
her to repeating these same three words. I had no idea what
they meant.

Airport security checkpoints are stressful. Add in a guard
yelling an incomprehensible reprimand, and hearts begin
to pound. I knew these words, but the tension of the situation muddled my brain. My husband, Mike, stood off to the
side, gathering our belongings as they reached the end of the
conveyor belt. Our daughters, Emilia and Ivy, bounced around
him like ricocheting pinballs. I kept them in my periphery but
focused on the guard. I wanted to understand.

"*As crianças' mãos! As crianças' mãos!*" the guard repeated.

She held up a gloved hand and wagged her fingers. I remembered *crianças*. Children! *Crianças* meant children, and she was trying to tell me something about the children! I smiled as if I'd accomplished something great. The guard rolled her eyes but continued to hold her hand up. *The children's hands,* that was what she was saying. I looked to my daughters, still in the throes of the energy surge that occurs whenever they are told to stand still and be patient. They gleefully ran their fingers up and down the belt of metal rollers that kept luggage moving along.

"Girls, stop!" I barked. "Don't touch; keep your fingers off!" Despite the delay in comprehension, I again felt pleased with myself for understanding. The guard folded her arms across her chest and shook her head at me in disapproval.

My linguistic parenting failure took place at São Paulo's Guarulhos Airport, a massive operation. In the preceding few years, thirty-nine million travelers had passed through its terminals. I took solace in the fact that, of those thirty-nine million, surely I wasn't the worst one.

Twenty-four hours before, we'd caught a brief glimpse of the Everglades, where the heat and mosquitoes were suitable preparation for our upcoming two months in Brazil. My only regret from our time in Florida, which included an airboat ride, feeding alligators, and strolling around a dilapidated animal park (which I guess is the term for a facility that falls short of an actual zoo), was that we were drenched in sweat by the end of it. I knew that Brazil would induce profuse sweating, but I wanted to delay that state of discomfort as long as possible, and I absolutely did not want to begin fifteen hours of travel in such condition. After extensive travel, even low standards of hygiene are difficult to maintain, and I accept that I'm less than pleasant by the time we arrive at a destination, but I don't want to *begin* a journey that way. It makes it that much more difficult for me to tolerate my own body.

Despite the sweat and mosquito bites, our flight from Miami to São Paulo was a success, because it did not crash. The human capacity to complain about airline travel astonishes me. We grumble at delays, inattentive attendants, less than gourmet food, and people who recline their seats (but really, those people are assholes). What we forget is the wonder of traveling through the skies in a metal tube to reach another continent, all in a matter of hours. Imagine making such a journey by sea. Or never traveling at all. If the plane lands at its destination and no one dies along the way, the flight is a success.

Reaching the São Paulo airport, where I studied Portuguese signs whenever a moment allowed and eavesdropped to decipher the spoken language, marked completion of the longest leg of our journey, but we still had one more to go. Londrina, a university town of about half a million people in the north of the state of Paraná, where Brazilians enjoy both a small urban environment and a more relaxed pace than their big city contemporaries, is a one-hour flight inland, or roughly west, of São Paulo. We found Londrina through a home exchange website, where we glance at the world through the window of our laptops and look for possible swaps. We'd queried two-dozen listings in all corners of the globe, and a Brazilian family had responded with interest.

Our exchange partners were also a family of four with children the same ages as ours, six and eight at the time of travel. While we headed to bask in the Brazilian summer, with the intention of using their home as a base camp from which we'd explore other parts of the country, the Brazilian family headed to our home in Idaho, with the hopes of introducing their children to snow and a possible white Christmas. Leading up to the exchange, I kept an online dialogue with my Brazilian counterpart. We exchanged tips and recommendations for our home cities, asking questions as they arose.

Could you leave us some recommendations for churches? she asked. *We attend a contemporary Christian service.*

After a brief moment of panic because there is no subject about which I am less knowledgeable, followed by a phone call to friends who might have an idea of how to respond, I wrote back with two suggestions.

Thank you, she replied. *And what about you?*

I could have answered a million ways. *Sure, why don't you leave us similar suggestions.* Or, *No, thank you, we won't be attending services while in Brazil.* Either would have been acceptable. Instead, I typed back a weak and heathenish, *We're good.*

"Mom?" Emilia interrupted my thoughts as our plane began its descent to Londrina. "Will we get to play with the kids who live in the house we're staying at?"

"No, sweetie. They're already on their way to America."

"Oh. So we can play with them when we get back to our house in America?"

"No, we won't meet them at all. When we get back to America, they will already be on their way back to Brazil."

"So, we're never going to get to play with them?"

"Well, I don't know about *never.*" Though I knew full well that the answer was probably never. "But we're not going to meet them during this trip or when we return."

"Then why even go to Brazil?" she asked, as if our entire motivation to travel centered on playing with two specific children she'd never met and knew nothing about.

"Well, there are lots of reasons to go to Brazil. It's a huge country. We'll see the Amazon and Carnival and learn about Brazilian food and culture. It's going to be awesome."

"Be honest, Mom. You just want to see a sloth."

"Okay, I really do want to see a sloth, but there will be some things that we all enjoy. There will be a pool where we're staying. And you know, there are other kids in Brazil, too."

"I guess," she said.

"Mom?" Ivy had been eavesdropping from her spot across the aisle next to Mike. "What kinds of treats do you think they have in Brazil?"

"I don't know, Ivy. But I bet they have many different kinds of treats, and I bet they're all yummy."

She turned to her father and whispered, "I'm really excited about the treats."

We landed (and no one died, another success), disembarked, and the Londrina airport reminded me of the Boise airport. Quaint, manageable, and nothing like the monstrosities of São Paulo or LAX.

"Do we know what this person looks like?" Mike asked. Our exchange partners had arranged for a neighbor to pick us up at the airport, just as we had arranged for them in Boise.

"No, but I think she's going to have a sign. And something tells me our family of four is going to be easy to spot." With our excess of luggage, blonde and blue-eyed daughters, and general look of displacement and confusion, we held no resemblance to our Brazilian fellow travelers.

"Amanda?" Sure enough, we were spotted as soon as we emerged from baggage claim. A tall, pretty woman held a small sign with our names on it.

"Yes." I smiled.

"Oh, God bless you. I am Silvana. Welcome, welcome. God bless you. You made it. God *bless* you." After introductions, our hostess blessed us further and took us on a brief driving tour of Londrina's main streets.

Emilia, Ivy, and I sat in the back. "Mom, what's a sex shop?" Emilia asked as we stopped at a red light.

"*So*," Mike said, a little too loudly, attempting to direct our driver's attention away from Emilia's inquiry, "what's the weather like this time of year?"

While Silvana detailed the forecast for Mike—intense heat interrupted by an occasional afternoon thunderstorm—I followed Emilia's gaze to two storefronts labeled "Sex Shop" and "Sexy Shop." One was decorated with the word "HOT" in shiny red letters and a heart in the same material. The heart looked more suited to Valentine's decorations in an elementary school classroom than an enticement to shop for lube. I wondered if the Sexy Shop was sexier than the mere Sex Shop. Was the addition of the *y* an attempt at one-upmanship? To be fair, there was nothing unsavory about the street upon which we drove, and both shops were surrounded by restaurants, pharmacies, and a pet shop. I pounced on the latter as a means of avoiding Emilia's question.

"Oh, look. A pet store! Look at the puppies!"

Emilia glared at me with narrowed eyes. At the age of eight, she was getting harder to misdirect.

"But you never want us to look at pets because you said we can't have pets and you don't think the dogs should be in tiny cages," she countered with suspicion.

"Well, that's true," I said. The light turned green, and our discussion of sex shops and pet stores mercifully fizzled.

"And here is Igapo Lake," our guide said as we crossed a small bridge. Walking paths stretched on either side.

"Oh, look at the water," Ivy said with her nose pressed to the glass.

"And now we are not far." While Silvana spoke in impeccable English, I could tell that doing so was difficult, and I appreciated her effort. She drove us to the gated community in which we'd be staying, though *gated* was an understatement. Atop massive walls sat coils of barbed wire, over which stretched an electric fence. I wondered how much of the neighborhood armor was put to the test and how much was just for show. At the gate, Silvana punched a code into a keypad. A traffic-blocking arm swung up in front of us, but a further gate, more substantial, remained closed. Our driver turned to a security booth and smiled and waved before this gate relented and permitted us entry.

"After we get you settled into the house," she said, "we will go to the security booth and get you your own code to use during your stay."

We entered our temporary home to find it exactly as it had been pictured on the exchange website. Mike and Silvana made their way back to the security guard to procure us a code while the girls and I dragged our suitcases inside and looked around.

"Did you get a code?" I asked Mike upon his return.

"Yeah," he said. "Not just a code to get in and out of the community but also an alternate distress code to use if I'm under duress."

"Wow."

"No kidding."

"Are you going to tell me what it is?" I asked.

"If I do, are you accidentally going to punch in the distress code because you'll be trying so hard not to?"

"It's possible," I admitted. My fingers, almost Tourettic in nature, are entirely capable of such a blunder. "I'll just try to not get kidnapped."

A knock at the door revealed our friendly neighborhood shepherd had returned for a few last words. "If there is anything you need, Amanda," Silvana said, "please call me, and I will do what I can to help you."

"Okay, and thank you so much," I said. "Thank you for meeting us at the airport, for everything. We really appreciate it."

"God bless you, Amanda. God bless your family. God bless you. God bless you. God bless you."

She could not have been kinder and had somehow deduced that I was in need of a great many blessings.

"You, too," I finally said. "And thanks again."

She departed, and we began the laborious task of unpacking and the more enjoyable endeavor of exploring our new home. It was large and modern, with a giant brick wall on one side of the living room and a glass-walled staircase leading to the upstairs bedrooms. A large back patio included an extra sitting area and outdoor kitchen. I looked through the main kitchen, trying to identify the basic means of making ice, drinkable water, and coffee. Our exchange partners had graciously left us wine, soft drinks, and lasagna so that we could forgo a trip to the store after our many hours of travel. I thought of my own kitchen back in Boise, where I'd left gifts for the children on the counter but not much in the way of food.

The Brazilian kitchen seemed small to me, until I reminded myself that it was more than adequate, but I'd grown accustomed to the grossly oversized amenities so popular in the United States.

A colony of tiny ants, almost cute save for the fact that they were infesting a kitchen, crawled along the countertops. I would spend days trying to eradicate them before admitting that this wasn't possible and the best I could hope for was peaceful coexistence.

After a few minutes of snooping, I called to Mike, "There aren't any knives."

"What do you mean there aren't any knives?" he hollered back from the living room. "I'm sure they have knives."

"Well, they have butter knives. But there aren't any cutting knives."

"There must be," he said, joining me in the kitchen.

We searched the drawers repeatedly to no avail.

"That doesn't make any sense," Mike said. "Wait, what's back here?"

Behind a propped door hid a small pantry. On a high shelf sat a large, oval serving dish, on the outside of which was a taped sign that read "Caution!!" Mike pulled the dish out and sat it on the counter. This was the home of all cutting knives, scissors, a can opener, and a corkscrew.

"Well, that's different," Mike said. "How old are their kids?"

"Same as ours, six and eight."

"I wonder what they think of our kitchen in Boise," he said.

"Oh dear." I had images of everything within reach of children: cutting knives, scissors, corkscrews, can openers, barbecue skewers, graters, julienne slicers, and electric dicers. "Well, I'm sure they'll move things as they see fit." I looked at the caution sign again with its double exclamation points. "Between this and the security guard at the São Paulo airport,

I get the feeling that Brazilians are really afraid that our kids are going to lose a finger while they're here."

"No one is going to cut off a finger," Mike reassured me.

"You're right." I relaxed my shoulders, weary of talk of knives, happy that we'd made it safely to Brazil.

"After all," he continued, "we're far more likely to have a finger bitten off by a piranha."

* * *

Brontosaurus for Dinner

*Completely unsurprisingly, the survey revealed that the three most
commonly consumed foodstuffs of Brazil are rice, beans and coffee . . .
Next in line in terms of favorite foods in Brazil are bread and beef.*

—Flavors of Brazil

Of all the things I wanted to do in Brazil, dying was not
one of them. Not just because of the obvious negatives
of death itself but also because it would be a terrible inconvenience for my family. I could only imagine Mike, with his
sparse knowledge of Portuguese, trying to wade through the
bureaucratic barriers to transporting a body out of Brazil and
into the United States. Such an endeavor was likely to be, as
my mother would have declared, "a royal pain in the ass."

"I don't want to be a pain in your ass, honey," I whispered
to Mike.

"What? What are you talking about?"

"Remember, I want to be cremated. It'll be so much easier.
You can just take my ashes in your carry-on."

"You're not dying."

"Also, I don't remember where I put our wills."

"Stop talking, and take these." He shoved a handful of

ibuprofen and a glass of water in my face. It was our second day in Brazil, and I had a fever of 103°. I was pretty sure death was forthcoming but took the pills anyway.

I dozed throughout the day, in my waking moments trying to remember details of dengue and malaria, so that if I did pull through, I'd have some idea of what lasting damage awaited me. Despite our use of insect repellant, we'd all suffered mosquito bites. I knew that even if I had been bitten by a mosquito carrying malaria or dengue, it would take more than a day for symptoms to show. On the other hand, I'd always been an overachiever, so the wait time was probably less in my case.

The Zika virus was gaining widespread attention at the time of our arrival in Brazil, like an unfortunate welcoming gift. As my fever slowly abated and I accepted the fact that I might survive, I researched Zika with feelings of gratitude that I was not pregnant, trying to get pregnant, or capable of getting anyone else pregnant. I'm grateful for these things at all times, but reading about the Zika virus made them extra special.

"So, what do you think I had?" I asked Mike, once I was clearly on the mend. "Dengue, malaria, or Zika?"

"I think you had a twenty-four-hour flu."

"Because really, how would I know which one? I mean each of them give you flu-like symptoms and then in most cases go away."

"I really just think you had a flu."

"Or maybe I had all three. Or *have* all three, because you know they stick with you even when the symptoms subside."

"It's time to go," Mike said, signifying that not only was it time to go but also that he'd had enough of my hypochondria for one day.

"Okay," I agreed. "I'll begin the ridiculously long process of getting our children to put on shoes."

We were headed back to the Londrina airport. Not to depart in fear of viruses but to retrieve my in-laws, who were joining us for a few weeks. After asking the girls a mere six times to use the bathroom and put on their shoes, we herded them out the door and into a small SUV in the driveway. In addition to exchanging homes, we'd agreed to exchange vehicles. Long-term travel becomes far more affordable when those pesky details like accommodations and transportation are bartered rather than purchased.

"You got this," I said to Mike. Whenever we drive in a foreign country, also known as "Mike driving in a foreign country," I try to help by offering words of encouragement. This does more harm than good, because when Mike is navigating new territory, he'd prefer I remain silent, speaking up only to help with directions when needed. That doesn't mean I can stop myself. "No problem. Piece of cake. You *so* got this." Mike can drive on either side of the road and from either side of the vehicle. He can adapt to almost any conditions to get us safely to our destination. Brazil promised to be easily manageable; he wouldn't have to drive on the other side of the road or from the other side of the car, as he had on our previous trip to Australia. Brazil did, however, offer a more lackadaisical approach to following rules of the road. Brazilian motorists view traffic lanes, lights, and signs as guidelines rather than absolutes.

The route from our home in Londrina to the airport was an easy one. Points A and B were on opposite ends of the town but connected by only four major roads and no highway travel. I consulted a large map in my lap.

"Okay, so you have to go right at this first street but then just down to the roundabout and turn around so we can head the other way," I said. "And it's Avenida Madre Leônia Milito, so obviously we'll use Billy Joel to remember that one."

"We will?"

"Mama Leone left a note on the door? Billy Joel?"

"Yeah, I got nothing," he said.

"We're going to make a left at the roundabout onto Higienópolis. And that's just fun to say, so that will be easy to remember."

"You know, I really only need to drive this route once, and then I'll have it down. I'm not too worried about remembering street names."

"I know, but what if *I* need to remember them? What if I'm driving to the airport by myself?"

Mike said nothing and made the turn onto Higienópolis. We both knew that chances didn't favor me driving in Brazil. I'm a competent driver but not a calm one.

"Look, Emilia, there's the lake," Ivy said.

"Man, I hope we get to go fishing," Emilia said.

"My next right is JK, yes?" Mike asked.

"Yes. That one will definitely be easy to remember." It wasn't a Harry Potter tribute, though that is the association that would make it memorable for us. JK was how the Londrinese referred to the avenue named for Juscelino Kubitschek, a deceased former president credited as "the father of modern Brazil." JK (the avenue, not the man) led to Santos Dumont, which dead-ended at the airport.

"I can't wait to see Nana and Papa," Ivy said as we exited the car and crossed the parking lot to the airport under brilliant sunshine.

"Me, too," I agreed. While I looked forward to visiting with my in-laws, I also didn't yet feel fully recuperated from my twenty-four-hour flu, also known as the plague that had ripped through my body and that I'd miraculously survived. If I took another downturn, my in-laws would step in to help and, if needed, care for the children while Mike dealt with the hassle of getting my ashes ready for a return trip to America.

We arrived at the airport early, so we stopped at a small, second-floor café for a snack. In truth, no one was hungry, but we had time to kill, and I was dying to order a cheese bun. One of the first phrases I'd learned in Portuguese was how to order a *pão de queijo*, or cheese bun. When I ordered, the waitress understood me on the first try, and I felt redeemed from my interaction with security in São Paulo. If Mike could get us where we were going and I could order us cheese buns along the way, our trip was destined for success. The cheese bun, or cheese bread as it translates, was not exactly the decadent, cheese-filled bread I'd hoped for but more interesting than your average dinner roll. Cheese is mixed into dough made of tapioca flour and baked into light little puffs of snacking goodness.

"That's okay, Mom," Emilia said after a nibble. "I'm not really hungry."

"Me neither," said Ivy.

"They're not great," Mike added.

The three of them returned their cheese buns to the plate, at which point I ate everyone else's. I didn't love them, but I am a mom, and at some point in my early motherhood journey, I accepted that one of my duties as a mother is to act as a human garbage disposal.

"Okay, but listen, guys," I said to my family. "We are not giving up on cheese buns yet. There are very few things I can order, and *pão de queijo* is one of them. Besides, you can't judge something on the airport version of it. I bet if we bought these in a real bakery, they'd be awesome."

We returned to the first level and the area into which passengers would emerge after baggage claim. My daughters love to meet people at the airport. In fact, so do I. Not just because it typically signifies a reunion after geographical separation but also because I find nothing more depressing than people arriving at an airport with no one to greet them.

As exciting as it is to greet arrivals, both Emilia and Ivy grow profoundly disappointed at anyone who walks through the arrivals door who is not the person they are there to greet. It's as if every other passenger exists as a personal affront.

"That's not Nana," Ivy said as a tall woman in tight jeans, four-inch heels, and a plunging neckline emerged.

"No, that is not Nana," Mike confirmed.

"And that's not Nana *or* Papa," Emilia said in response to a young couple who managed to walk with considerable luggage while each kept a hand firmly in the back pocket of their partner's jeans.

After the passage of another three-dozen people who, in Emilia and Ivy's eyes, were all guilty of the crime of *not* being Nana and Papa, their beloved grandparents arrived. Both girls rushed to them with hugs and shouts, and Nana presented each with a lollipop, as she is known to do.

"You made it," I said to my father-in-law and gave him a hug. This is one of the most-uttered phrases at an airport, as if we all secretly harbor the concern that our friends and family won't actually make it.

"Yes," my father-in-law said. "Though I kind of made a mess on the plane. They gave us this little salad with the meal, and when I went to pour on the salad dressing, I didn't see that there was plastic wrap stretched over the top of the salad."

"Yes," my mother-in-law chimed in as she helped Ivy unwrap her lollipop. "So that happened."

"Oh, Dad," Mike said.

"I wasn't wearing my glasses."

"Well, welcome to Brazil," I offered. "Let's go see the house."

The six of us piled into the SUV and retraced our route back to the home in the gated community.

"This looks really nice," my mother-in-law said. The street our borrowed home was on sloped down, flanked by modern townhomes, manicured lawns, and flowering hibiscus trees.

"Wow," my father-in-law said as we led them inside the house. "Sometimes that home exchange thing you do really works out, doesn't it?"

"Sometimes it does," Mike agreed.

That evening, we settled on Costelaria Jardim, a nearby restaurant that promised not only live music but also a kids' club, so it seemed to have something for everyone. A lush, green canopy shielded an outdoor patio but wasn't enough to stop a determined drizzle, so we sat inside at a long table under a television monitor. Overhead, Rod Steward, Elton John, and Billy Joel crooned away in a series of 1980s music videos.

The restaurant's signature dish, the Brontosaurus, was the largest cut of meat I have ever seen cooked and served in a restaurant. It's smaller than the sides of beef you've seen Sylvester Stallone punching in the meat locker scene in

Rocky, but only by a little. Placemats showed a diagram of the Brontosaurus, which was comprised of multiple cuts of meat, cooked and served as one cut before the butcher could separate them out into different steaks. The placemat told you where on the Brontosaurus you would find the filet, the sirloin, or the rump, so you knew where to focus if you had designs on a certain cut. It was ostentatious, excessive, and barbaric.

"Let's get the Brontosaurus," Mike said.

"And the ribs," added my father-in-law.

"Man," Emilia said, "Brazil is like Meat Land." After a moment she reconsidered. "No, it's like Meat Heaven."

"I wonder if they have any kind of salad." I flipped to the back of the menu and found a picture of a plate of tomato slices topped with onions.

"It's like Meatopia!" Emilia declared.

When the waiter approached and asked us a question, all eyes turned immediately to me, and I accepted my role as our half-assed, almost-competent translator. I ordered the meaty obscenity, its rib accompaniment, the tomatoes, and a round of caipirinhas, Brazil's national drink.

"Can we go see the playroom now?" Ivy asked.

"We can check it out," I said with a fair dose of apprehension. We walked a short hallway and peered into a small room equipped with toys for toddlers, a television, coloring pages, and crayons. "There's no one here. Why don't you guys stay with us for a little a bit, and then maybe later there will be some other kids here."

"But I want to go in," Ivy said.

A woman who worked at the restaurant approached, entered the room, and beckoned the girls in.

"See, Mom. It's open!" Emilia said.

I smiled at the woman and told her that my daughters did not speak Portuguese. She smiled back and opened a translation app on her phone. After typing for a moment, she showed the screen to Emilia, who read, "What is your name?" and then answered, "Emilia. My name is Emilia."

"Emilia," the woman repeated back, then motioned to a piece of paper and the crayons.

Emilia would write a question, and the woman would translate with her phone and write the answer in English on the paper. Before we left that evening, the woman gave me the transcript. The two struck up a conversation, during which Emilia asked a host of inappropriate questions like, "Do you have a husband?" "Why don't you have a husband?" and "Are you ever going to have a husband?"

Ivy busied herself with crayons and coloring pages. When I checked on them later, I found her engrossed in an episode of *Peppa Pig* in Portuguese. At first glance, I'd thought the playroom would be a no-go, but the girls had a wonderful time and would only return to the table to eat with much prompting. When they rejoined us, they were delighted to find that entrees in Brazil are almost always delivered with heaping plates of white rice and french fries.

"I was worried this place was closed when we first walked in, because there was hardly anybody here," I said. "But now it seems to be filling up." Diners trickled in, and a musician set up his equipment as our meal came to an end.

"I'm sure they eat much later here," Mike said.

"Right," I agreed. "They'll probably be slammed at ten o'clock tonight."

"Can we please go back to the playroom?" Ivy asked. "I'm missing *Peppa Pig*."

"But it's in Portuguese," I pointed out. "You don't even know what they're saying."

"Yes, I do. I've seen it before."

"Then why do you want to see it so bad?" Mike asked.

"Ugh, *Dad*." She rolled her eyes in exasperation, as if it was a terrible burden suffering the company of such dense adults.

"I'll walk you girls back to the playroom," Nana offered, then turned to me, "if Mommy orders us one more round."

"Deal," I said, followed by a silent prayer of thanks that I have the coolest mother-in-law on the planet.

The guitarist began his set, and though we couldn't understand the words, the universality of music carried the experience. Before long, my slightly tipsy in-laws stood up and started dancing. The wait staff gathered around to watch in appreciation.

I held Mike's hand under the table and felt content. Everyone had arrived safely, we had a successful outing, and I relaxed into acceptance that this wasn't so hard and I just might survive. We'd soon set out for other locations in Brazil, but my confidence was high. I was sure we could do this. What could go wrong?

* * *

Personal Rain Cloud

It's called passenger shaming, or the act of taking travelers—
usually air travelers—to task for their boorish behavior.

—Christopher Elliot, *USA Today*

"We have a major problem."

"This is bad," Mike agreed.

"Very bad."

"We still have our credit cards. At least they work."

We'd tried five cash machines with no luck. I'd informed the bank of our travels, and we had money in our account, but time and time again, I was denied when trying to access it.

"The tour companies only take cash," I said.

"What? How can that be?"

"I don't know. It's just a Brazil thing, I guess."

We would depart later that afternoon for a flight to Manaus, where we'd be met by a tour operator who would rightfully expect to be paid. Cash was critical.

We finally resorted to the all-knowing, sometimes-lying resource that I both love and hate. My very best frenemy, the Internet.

"It says here that only certain ATMs will permit transactions with cards originating outside of Brazil," I reported, "and these ATMs are most likely to be attached to a Citibank, HSBC, or Banco do Brasil."

With the understanding that we simply hadn't been going to the right cash machines, I looked up locations of multiple branches of Citibank, HSBC, and Banco do Brasil and marked them on our city map. Mike's parents watched the girls while my husband and I began a journey around Londrina to banks where money couldn't be withdrawn due to power outages, banks where money couldn't be withdrawn because they were out of money, and banks where money couldn't be withdrawn because the banks didn't actually exist (the Internet lies).

"We're running out of options," Mike said, pulling up to yet another Citibank.

"This one is going to work," I said. "I can feel it."

"Let's hope so," Mike said. The bank appeared to have electricity and hopefully had cash to dispense. "If it does work, take out the maximum."

He waited with the car, unsure if we were legally parked or not, while I successfully withdrew cash, almost shouting "Hallelujah!" once I'd done so.

"It worked?" he asked when I returned to the car smiling.

"Yes!"

"How much did you get?"

"Five hundred reals."

"What? That's not enough. That's like 125 bucks. What if we have this much trouble finding an ATM in Manaus? I think you should go back and do another withdrawal."

"I can't. They have daily limits. This one would only let me take out five hundred."

"That's no good."

"Yeah, but at least we have something."

"Before we go back, I want to make one more stop to get your phone squared away." Mike was determined to get my phone working with a local SIM card, which I appreciated, as it kept me connected to e-mail when firing up the laptop wasn't an option, but dealing with phone companies is similar to dealing with banks. Good experiences are possible, but so are maddening ones involving long waits, misunderstandings, and malfunctions. These errands, involving the aspects of money and technology during travel, are my least favorite. We survived, but only after an hour of sweating in a crowded room, shoulder to shoulder with other customers ranging from the hopeful to the irate, each of us clutching a small piece of paper on which a number signified the order in which we'd be helped.

"We'd better hurry," I said as we left the store and jogged back to the car. We had to relieve my in-laws of their babysitting duties, and then everyone had to pack and prepare for our flight to Manaus.

"Yeah," Mike agreed. "That took about ten times longer than I'd hoped."

"Do you know what the Brazilian motto is?" I asked.

"No, should I?"

"It's 'Brazil: An exercise in patience.'"

"You're making that up," he challenged.

"Yeah," I admitted. "It's actually 'Order and Progress.' That's what it says on their flag, *Ordem E Progresso.* But I like my version better."

* * *

"And we need to see the children's birth certificates," the gate agent said. He spoke perfect English.

"What?" I'd heard him correctly; I just didn't understand. My in-laws eyed me nervously from the next counter where they were checking themselves in with little problem.

"You cannot fly with the children without their birth certificates."

We were back at the Londrina airport. I'd just handed the agent four passports, for Mike, me, and both of our daughters. Each of those passports had a Brazilian visa stapled inside of it, a visa that had required furnishing multiple forms and original documents (including our children's birth certificates) to the Brazilian consulate, along with a sizable chunk of cash. I'd assumed that having gone through the tedious and expensive task of obtaining visas would be good enough. I hadn't thought to then also bring their birth certificates.

"But they have visas," I said. "We had to show the birth certificates to the consulate to get the visa." The gate agent shook his head as if he was merely doing what he had to do in keeping with his job and in the interest of curbing human trafficking. He took our passports and conferred with the gate agent who'd been helping my in-laws.

What did this mean? All of our domestic flights in Brazil were now forfeited? Were Manuas, Rio, Salvador, and São Paulo now taken off the itinerary? Did this mean they wouldn't let us go when it was time to leave the country? Should we start assimilating into Brazilian culture for the long haul? What did this mean for my in-laws? Would they gallivant around Brazil without us? The two gate agents finished their conference. My in-laws' agent was handing Nana and Papa their boarding passes. I looked to our agent.

"It's fine," he said, then handed us our boarding passes as if the prospect of not letting us board had been a minor and easily remedied glitch. Perhaps he toyed with tourists for his own amusement. Sadist.

"Oh, okay," I said, fearful that we might have the same problem trying to leave another Brazilian city.

My in-laws were still chatting and laughing with their gate agent while Mike and I quickly herded our girls away from ours, lest he change his mind and revert to asking for birth certificates again.

"And you get preferred boarding," the other agent said to Mike's parents, "because of your *age*."

We didn't have a direct flight to Manaus and would first return to São Paulo for a two-and-a-half-hour layover. As we boarded the plane (long after my in-laws took advantage of their preferred boarding because of their *age*), we found clouds of white air spewing forth from the plane's vents. Poisoned gas, surely.

When we disembarked in São Paulo, I grabbed my backpack from the overhead bin and noticed that it was damp. I assumed it was from the condensation, which I no longer feared was poisoned gas, as all of the passengers still seemed to be very much alive.

"I think something leaked," Mike said when he retrieved his backpack from overhead.

"Mine is damp, too," I said. "I think it's just from all the condensation."

"You're probably right."

We didn't think anything more of it and passed the hours in the São Paulo airport with beer, Oreos, and one tedious game of Uno, with the cards awkwardly perched on my lap.

We boarded the plane for Manaus, and when all was settled, it began to rain. Not outside but inside the plane, and just over me, as if my personal rain cloud was determined to have its influence on my travel experience. I don't mind being rained on, but I do mind an entire plane watching and only *me* getting rained on. I caught the rain in the curve of the inflight magazine to keep it from soaking my seat, then flagged down a flight attendant. She opened the overhead compartment and identified a bag as the culprit of dripping water. It was my bag, home to a water bottle with a lid that hadn't been screwed on tight. I wanted nothing more at that moment than to disown our belongings, but I could not. So I did the next best thing. I took the bag from the flight attendant's hands and immediately passed it across the aisle to Mike.

An hour into the flight, I was sure the problem was behind me. I was correct; I heard a man three rows back complain that water was leaking on him. The upward trajectory of the plane had pushed the remaining water in the overhead bin further down the line. Maybe the ban of water on flights in America wasn't for antiterrorism. Maybe it was to keep idiots like me from unintentionally annoying other passengers.

We arrived in Manaus at two o'clock in the morning. Mike's face held a frightening pallor. He'd acquired my earlier illness and spent both flights huddled with nausea and feverish chills. Also disconcerting, I worried how my daughters would handle having to function in the middle of the night. Would there be meltdowns and tantrums and condemnation of us as parents for torturing them with sleep deprivation?

"Are you girls okay?" I asked them as we trudged off the plane.

"Yeah," said Emilia.

"This is fun," said Ivy.

"Aren't you two tired?" I asked.

"Mom, we're going to the Amazon. This is no time to be tired," Emilia said.

"So, you're sure someone is going to meet us?" Mike asked. Both he and my in-laws walked with an air of apprehension.

"Someone is supposed to be here. Just look for a sign with my name on it," I assured them. We'd been warned of expensive transportation schemes. To avoid clients like us falling victim, the Amazon tour company I'd contacted assured us that someone would be at the airport waiting for us.

"We're arriving an hour later than scheduled," my mother-in-law said. "I hope they're still here."

"Well, they asked for our flight information, so they should be taking the delay into account." At least I hoped so. We had no hotel booked, no address to go to. We were arriving with two small children in the middle of the night in the most populous city of Amazonas. All on the assurance by e-mail of someone we'd never met, spoken with, or given a deposit to. "Just look for someone with a sign with my name on it," I said again, more to reassure myself than anyone else. "I'm sure everything will be just fine."

"Mike Turner?"

We looked up to see a tall Brazilian holding a sign with my husband's name on it. "You have got to be kidding me," I muttered.

Mike whispered a quick, "Everything is going to be okay," before shaking hands with the driver who'd been sent to retrieve us. My husband had scheduled all Airbnb bookings during the trip, while I'd been the main point of contact for our exchange partners. I'd also handled *all* correspondence with the tour company. For months, I'd worked diligently to arrange our Amazon adventure. Every e-mail had come from my account, signed with my name. Amanda Turner. I had made this happen, yet when it came time to greet our group at the airport, they'd subordinated me to my husband. The feminist in me was pissed. This emotion was countered with gratitude that at least someone was there to meet us.

Our driver spoke little English but successfully communicated that he was going to take us to the tour office. We piled into his van, and I wondered what sort of tour office was open at two o'clock in the morning. The company had been well rated on the Internet, but maybe that was all a scam and we were now entering the dark and seedy world of human trafficking. Or was this an elaborate mugging? Despite my fears, the driver took us to a small tour office in downtown Manaus just blocks from the city's famed opera house. There, a man with impeccable English greeted us as if it was three in the afternoon, with no signs of fatigue or indication that meeting in the middle of the night was out of the ordinary.

"Hey, guys," he said, "so here's the deal. I'm going to take you to a hotel just a few doors down. You can get a few hours of sleep and then meet me back here at seven in the morning. Sound good?" We nodded and did as he said, following him to a hotel three doors down. "This hotel is not the best," he warned. "It's pretty rough, but this way you're real close and there's no chance of you getting lost. Plus, it's only for a few hours." He then switched to Portuguese to secure us two rooms.

"He wasn't kidding when he said it was rough," I said as we opened the door to our room a few minutes later. We couldn't see anything, but there was a general air of decay about the building.

"Let's just concern ourselves with getting the light on," Mike said. The switch on the wall didn't work. "I found a breaker box."

"Are you sure you should be messing with that?" I asked.

"Mom, why can't I come in the room?" Emilia said.

"It's too dark. Let Dad try to get the lights working first."

"I think the lights just don't work," he said. "Start thinking of how you're going to communicate that to the woman downstairs."

"I don't think she's downstairs," I said. "I think as soon as she handed us the keys, she locked the front door and went to bed."

"You're right," he said. "Do we *need* light?"

"I'll try and find the flashlights."

"Oh, wait. Uh, never mind." The lights came on as Mike took the small wooden block that served as a keychain and slid it into a sensor on the wall. This is a common practice in hotels outside the U.S. Turning the lights on requires the key, so that guests can't lock up and leave with the lights still on. "Wow. We are really dumb."

"No, blame it on three o'clock in the morning."

With the lights on, the full glory of the room came into focus. Wires hung from the ceiling over two thin mattresses on plywood. A hole in the bathroom wall gave a perfect view of the night sky.

"This hotel is fun!" Ivy said.

"Is this our bed?" Emilia asked, indicating the smaller of the two.

"Yes," I nodded, "but this is not the time for fun. This is the time for sleep. We only have four hours before we have to get up and go back to the tour office."

"But I want to play," Ivy protested. "I like this place."

When everyone was in bed and the lights were off, intentionally so, I whispered to Mike, "We have stayed in some shitty hotel rooms in our time, but I think this one might actually be the shittiest."

"Yes," he agreed.

"But there is a silver lining."

"That we're only here for four hours?"

"That, too. But I was thinking about the fact that it doesn't smell bad."

"You're right. It doesn't smell bad."

"Think of all the hotel rooms we've stayed in where it smelled like there was a body decaying under the bed."

"Do I have to?" he asked.

"You're right. That's a bad idea; don't think of decaying bodies."

"Well it's too late now."

"Sorry," I said. "Sweet dreams."

* * *

Welcome to the Jungle

Talking about of our own Lodge, please do not have also a big expectation we have private shower, private toilet fan protection agains insect through the windows but please do not expect luxury .

—Amazon Gero Tours Manaus

The next morning, we checked out of our shabby accommodations and headed for the tour office. We found the same employee there who had met us in the middle of the night. The office was small and the hub for what would prove to be a logistically impressive operation. Different groups of tourists and adventurers wandered in and out, some bound for the jungle lodge, others embarking on boat tours.

There is a mystique about the Amazon that draws people to it. Maybe it has to do with the mass of the river and its tributaries that number over a thousand, home to river dolphins, piranha, electric eels, and species yet undiscovered. Or the scope of a rain forest with 390 billion trees in over fifteen thousand species. For some, the draw is in the fact that this landscape is changing and that those numbers will be whittled down over time into figures easier to wrap your head around. There is an urgency to visit all the wondrous places before we destroy them, to walk in the home of jaguars and anacondas, macaws and howler monkeys, and millions of insect species. Or, more likely, the intrigue of the Amazon is due to the 1997 movie *Anaconda,* with great lines like "I'm not your bloody poodle!" and "You get the privilege of hearing your bones break before the power of embrace causes your veins to explode."

In any case, we found ourselves among the curious. We were adventurous enough to want to journey on the river and into the jungle but not stupid enough to do so without a guide. The price we'd been quoted was three hundred dollars per person. That included the transportation from the airport, for which we'd been grateful at two o'clock in the morning, transportation to the jungle lodge, five nights' lodging, and all meals. It seemed like an incredible deal, almost too much so, and as people filed in and out of the tour office, and I waited my turn to settle up, I feared that the price, now that we were in Manaus with no other plans, would suddenly increase. This fear is common when traveling, the sinking feeling that you are about to be scammed or about to find out that you've already been scammed. It happens because most of us have been scammed at one point, and the fear lingers and carries over to other situations.

In the case of Amazon Gero Tours, the office in which I stood nervously, afraid of impending extortion, I could not have been dealing with a more reputable and upstanding company. The cost was as quoted. The tour company was also familiar with the fact that, as foreigners, obtaining money from a cash machine can be a difficult and complicated process, and the staff made several trips that morning, driving their clients to an ATM that worked for cards originating outside of Brazil.

When we'd paid and were ready to begin our Amazon experience, we were directed to a van waiting across the street. We boarded, joining two other travelers already seated, an Australian and a Dane. Then we waited—and then waited some more. A group of four Americans, all in their early twenties, delayed the van. When they finally boarded, in a barrage of profanity and oblivious to (or unconcerned with) the presence of my children, we marveled at their gear. They were decked out like a North Face mannequin.

Our van ride was half an hour to the port of Manaus, an important place for commercial operations ranging from giant oceangoing vessels stacked with shipping containers to the smaller boats shuttling tourists like ourselves across to Careiro, from where we'd venture further into the Amazon. We got off the bus and found, as in many ports, vendors selling all manner of items, from candy to fish.

I took both girls by the hand, and we made our way along a narrow sidewalk that flanked a large, paved slope into the Rio Negro. Vehicles of all manner backed down the slope to launch boats, retrieve boats, and unload cargo. It was a massive, chaotic operation where every vehicle seemed determined to have a near miss with those around it. While my attention was on the vehicles, fearing that we'd witness a horrific accident, the girls marveled at rows of iced fish in grays and browns and oranges, with eyes wide and gaping mouths (the fish, not my daughters).

"Oh my God, this is scary," I said, in response to the trucks and their boat trailers coming within inches of both vehicles and people.

"You're supposed to say, 'Oh my *gosh*,' Mom," Emilia reprimanded.

Our group made its way in a herd to a boat at the water's edge. We boarded, and I immediately settled our children and looked for children's life jackets among the many crammed into a gap in the roof of the small boat. The men in the group, from my husband and father-in-law to the young Americans (whom I'd since deduced were lawyers), did what men do in such situations. They look around to see if the other men are going to put their life jackets on, because no man wants to be the only man wearing a life jacket. This makes absolutely no sense to me, but I understand that it's wired into their DNA. After my kids were suited up, I grabbed a life jacket, put it on, and loudly proclaimed, "I've never been above wearing a life jacket, myself." One by one, the men reluctantly put their life jackets on until we were all properly suited up, with the exception of the captain and a young deckhand.

I had ammunition in forcing the life jacket issue, at least within my family. A few months before our departure, a prominent Boise attorney died when his boat capsized on a fishing trip in one of the Amazon tributaries. Boise was shocked to learn of the death of one of our own while abroad, and very few details emerged about the accident. I have no idea if the attorney was wearing a life jacket or not, but the recent tragedy made our group more inclined to err on the side of caution.

When I was fairly certain we'd survive the trip, the boat backed out into the water, jockeying for position at the crowded shore where others tried to do the same. We picked up speed when free of the crowded waters near the port, and I instinctively reached my hands out to put one on each of my children, as if the wind whipping my hair around might also scoop them up and carry them away.

We went first to the famed meeting of the waters. The captain let the boat idle while our guide explained the finer points of the phenomenon where the Rio Negro and the Rio Solimões meet. Because of differences in temperature and current, the dark waters of the Negro and the sandy-colored waters of the Solimões meet but don't mix. It appears as if a sloppy line has been drawn in between these waters, and the phenomenon is startling. We had the opportunity to put a hand in the water on either side of the meeting point to feel the differences in temperature.

After the meeting of the waters, the boat once again picked up speed and took us to Careiro, where we boarded a bus for a one-hour journey. Our guide informed us that he wouldn't be traveling further and was turning us over to a new guide, a young man who looked about fourteen years old and who I'd assumed was the deckhand.

"He doesn't speak English," our previous guide explained, "but he'll take care of you from here on." We bade our first chaperone farewell, and he returned to the boat for the trip back to Manaus.

During the one-hour bus ride, we stopped at a convenience store along the way where we could buy snacks and use a restroom.

"I need to stretch my legs," said my father-in-law.

"I need to use the bathroom," said my mother-in-law.

"I'll go buy some beer," I said, as it seemed like an appropriate accompaniment for our journey into the Amazon. "And a snack for the kids," I added guiltily.

At another stop along the way, five-gallon jugs of water were loaded into the bus, and at still another stop, a woman and a young girl boarded. I wasn't sure if they were hitching a ride or had a connection to the tour company. We drove farther and marveled at the trees and their notable waterlines, often looming twelve feet off the ground, and realized that many of the areas in which we were traveling spent a better part of the year submerged.

Eventually the bus reached its destination, a small port along one of the Amazon's tributaries. While the port in Manaus had bustled with ships of all sizes, commercial goods, and mammoth shipping containers, this was a small dock hosting a tiny store, with little fishing boats bobbing nearby.

"Can we get something from this store?" Ivy asked as soon as we'd disembarked from the bus and entered the miniscule market that sold snacks, beer, and fuel. "This looks like the best store ever. They have *everything!*" The store was one-tenth the size of a 7-Eleven in the U.S.

"Yes," Mike answered. "You can pick out a—" A loud *boom* cut him off; it sounded as if a crack of thunder had occurred directly overhead. A downpour emptied onto the tin roof of the small shack, and we peered out of a doorway to where the air had turned into sheets of pummeling water. The sound hadn't been thunder, merely the start of the rain. Amazonian skies don't ease into a downpour with an introductory trickle. Instead the rain falls with full force from the beginning.

"Are we going to have to get into the boat in this?" I whispered to Mike. Before he had a chance to answer, the rain stopped as abruptly as it had started.

We spent ten minutes making small talk with fellow travelers who would also be traveling by boat to the lodge, a string of questions including: Where are you from? What do you think the jungle lodge will be like? I wonder if we'll see . . . ? This last question ended in a dozen variations. Caiman?

Sloths? Toucans? Spiders? Snakes? Our musings were interrupted by the arrival of the two boats that would transport us. We piled in, our group of six and the Dane who'd traveled with us from Manaus, leaving the Australian and American walking REI ads to travel in the second boat. I was glad to have Luc, the Dane, in our boat, as he was fluent in Portuguese. We overloaded the small boats with luggage and bodies and tried to get comfortable on the wooden slats. We weighed the boats down enough that the sides hovered only an inch above the water, and I did my best to appear as if I wasn't terrified by the prospect of sinking at any moment.

Our boat driver, much like our previous guide, looked to be about fourteen years old and spoke no English, but he capably shuttled us along the meandering Amazonian tributary for thirty minutes. It was a spectacle of caiman and egrets, all of which were exotic to us passengers. Caiman are midsized crocodilians and what we would see the most of during that trip. They range in size from the length of a pencil to eight feet or more from snout to tail, and they basked in the sun along the shores or stayed submerged to keep cool, with only the distinctive reptilian eyes poking above the water. As we'd near those eyes, they'd silently descend and disappear.

"Holy shit," my mother-in-law muttered. This was in response to a large caiman, the biggest we would see on our trip. It basked in the mud along the shore, but as our boat passed by, it lunged in our direction, mouth wide and hissing. While the rest of us uttered collective "wows" and smiled with excitement, my mother-in-law attempted to stem leakage of bodily fluids. She has an intense aversion to (and fear of) reptiles. It doesn't matter what you tell her to overcome this, such as "snakes aren't really slimy" or "iguanas are vegetarians, they won't hurt you," her response is the same. "I don't care. I can't stand them. Get them away from me." The presence of caiman every fifteen feet along our journey unsettled her.

The boat continued along the shallow brown tributary, flanked on either side by tall green grasses under an intense blue sky, cleared of clouds after our earlier downpour, the landscape almost cartoon-like in its perfection. As the water level dwindled and grew ever more shallow, the boat periodically bottomed out, getting stuck on the river bottom. In response, the driver bounced the boat up and down until it maneuvered free. He raised the propeller to the highest it could go while still moving us forward, and puttered the boat until the water level prohibited advancing and we were forced to pull ashore. We unloaded ourselves and our gear and stood in the muddy marsh, waiting for the driver to lead the way. Instead, he gestured with his hand vaguely in one direction, which we took to mean that we were to start walking.

"Where do we go?" I asked Luc.

"He's telling us to go that way," he responded with the same vague gesture as the boat driver. We all looked at each other uncomfortably. The landscape was open fields of tall grasses and therefore less intimidating than if he'd let us off into thick jungle, but we could see no clear structure to head toward or path to follow, and we were less than confident at the prospect of being released into the wild marshes of the Amazon. Eventually the boat driver realized our discomfort and, instead of motoring away and stranding us, pulled his boat further ashore and began walking, barefoot through the mud, in front of us. We followed.

"Mom, how long do we have to walk for?" Emilia asked.

"I have no idea," I answered.

"Dad, how long do we have to walk for?" Ivy asked.

"I have no idea," Mike answered.

The girls looked at each other and then glanced at their Nana and Papa, as if debating if there was any merit in posing the question to them, but then shrugged their shoulders in resignation.

Under intense sun, the thick, humid air worked moisture into every article of clothing. The mud was slicker in some areas than others. There were times when we lost our footing and fell or almost fell, and other times when we stepped in camouflaged holes and found our legs sinking into mud up to our knees. The path was hidden in parts and led to narrow wooden boards that served as makeshift footbridges to scoot across, to keep from falling into bigger holes and patches of watery mud. Backpacks weighed us down, Mike and I shouldering the girls'. We were amazed that no one was in tears, and happy to carry a part of their load if that maintained everyone's pleasant demeanor. Because of the luggage we carried, there was no possibility of offering the girls piggyback rides along the way, nor any place to stop and rest, no dry patch of land on which to sit. After twenty minutes, we ached. We'd traveled for hours on two boats, a bus, and a van, all after four hours of sleep in the abominable hotel room. Clouds hovered, and I marveled at how quickly they'd taken their leave and reappeared.

"I think we should pick up the pace," said Luc. "It's going to rain."

He charged forth with what seemed like unreasonable panic. But then I remembered the earlier downpour, as well as the fact that Luc was the only member of our group who'd traveled throughout Brazil. If he panicked, it was likely merited.

"There's the lodge," my father-in-law said. I looked up to see a wooden structure high on a hill. A treacherous, narrow staircase with what looked like one hundred steps led from the marsh in which we walked up to the building. The treachery of the staircase wasn't due only to its steep incline with huge gaps between the slats but also because we all walked in shoes that were now two times their original sizes, caked with slick mud that clung determinedly.

When we finally reached the top of the staircase and the grounds of the jungle lodge, we were exhausted and covered in sweat, mud, mosquito bites, and sunburn. At the same time, there was a sense of adventure and accomplishment around us.

"Oh, look. My next group is here." A tall, slender, dark man with a Rastafarian hat greeted us. "I'm Sammy. I'll be your guide. Follow me." We followed Sammy along a wooden walkway that hovered a few feet above solid earth and grass, which was a welcome sight after forty-five minutes through marsh and mud. He seemed to read my mind. "Normally you wouldn't have that walk," Sammy said. "Normally the boat could bring you all the way up to the top of the stairs, but the rains haven't come yet. All that you walked will be under water when the rains come."

The walkway branched off in places, leading to small buildings along the left and right, but we continued straight to a much larger building, the main lodge. Sammy stopped short of entering. "You can set your stuff here and wash your shoes over there." We piled our backpacks into a heap and took turns scraping the mud from our shoes with a small scrub brush at an outdoor sink.

"Your rooms aren't ready yet, so just hang out here," he

instructed. And so our group huddled under the roof as the next downpour came.

"Rooms?" Mike asked. "I thought we were going to sleep in hammocks in the jungle."

"I'm not sure."

"I know we signed up for the cheapest option. Maybe they gave us an upgrade." The rain subsided, and Sammy handed out keys and showed my in-laws to their room, then Mike and I and the girls to another room where a queen-sized bed was flanked on either side by twin mattresses.

"Just drop off your things and then come to lunch," Sammy instructed.

"Lunch?" Mike asked.

"It feels like ten o'clock at night," I said. It was noon.

We gathered in the main room of the lodge, a dining hall where a buffet was set up and picnic tables were covered in plastic tablecloths. The buffet offered stews and vegetables, always accompanied by the ubiquitous beans and white rice. My in-laws joined us at a long table, and we all sighed with the relief of having made the journey to the lodge. We were a ragged, sweaty, tired lot.

"I can't believe how nice our room is," my father-in-law said. "I don't know what I expected, but seeing a real bed in there was a treat."

"Ours is the same," said Mike. "Much nicer than we thought it was going to be." In truth, the rooms had no air-conditioning, no towels, and a temporary halt on running water. But after the morning's trek, we'd set the bar for luxury low. A bed and a private toilet went a long way.

"Girls, what do you think of the Amazon so far?" my mother-in-law asked my daughters.

"It's good," said Emilia.

"I haven't seen a pink river dolphin yet," Ivy added. "But I did get a bug bite." As if the interaction with a mosquito was a fair trade for the lack of river dolphins thus far.

"Hey, guys." Sammy approached our table. "I put you in the wrong rooms. You were all supposed to be in the hammock room. I accidentally put you in their room." He motioned to the supremely outfitted twenty-something lawyers. "So I got it switched around. I'm sorry about that, but when you finish lunch, we gotta move you to the right room."

"Now it makes sense," I said to Mike.

After lunch, we gathered our belongings, relinquished our room keys, and followed Sammy further along the plank walkway until we reached a long rectangular building known as the hammock room. A tin, A-framed roof hovered over walls made of wood up to the waist and then screen up to the roofline. The two longer walls of the hammock room were dotted with hooks on which hammocks could be hung in a neat row, so that when you entered, you were faced with hammocks parallel to each other, in a line stretching the length of the building.

"Okay," Sammy said, "so you got six hammocks for you guys here." After the first six, I counted three additional hammocks, totaling nine of us that would be sharing the room that night. "And there's the shower, and there's the toilet." A small, reeking bathroom was home to the toilet, toilet paper, a showerhead coming from the wall, a fleet of moths decorating the walls, and a congress of spiders holding silent court. "And then of course there's the sink." He motioned to a small sink outside of the bathroom in the big hammock room, so that eight of us could at least wash our faces and brush our teeth while one of us laid claim to the shower and toilet room. "Of course, the water's not working right now."

"Do you have any idea when it will be on?" my mother-in-law asked.

"No."

"Are there any towels, in case the water does come back on?" I asked.

"We're running a little low on towels at the moment. I'll see if I can get you some, maybe tomorrow." I knew the lodge had bathrooms, so it had never occurred to me that after our sweaty, arduous trek, we wouldn't be able to shower. "Right now you have about ten minutes and then let's all meet by the bar."

"There's a bar?" My eyes lit up, and the question emerged from my lips with more enthusiasm than I'd planned.

"Yes, you walked past it at the top of the stairs. It's not open now, maybe later tonight. But let's meet there in about ten minutes, and we're going to go look for some river dolphins. Sound good?"

"Yes!" Ivy showed her excitement with a fist pump.

"I'll see you all there in just a little bit." Sammy left.

"Wow. River dolphins. Okay," said Mike with poorly hidden fatigue.

"I thought it was bedtime," my father-in-law said.

"It's two o'clock in the afternoon," Nana clarified.

We claimed our hammocks and set about reapplying deodorant, bug spray, and sunscreen. We gathered our water bottles to fill from a five-gallon jug in the main hall. As we prepared to exit the hammock room, a young couple entered and took down their two hammocks. Part of the jungle experience was the opportunity to take your hammock into the jungle and spend a night there, without the benefits of a roof, planked floors, and screens. We wished them luck.

When we met Sammy, he immediately began walking back down the steep staircase. We followed. At the bottom, he went back in the direction from which we came. We sank into both mud and the unwelcome knowledge that for every excursion on the water (and there were to be many), we would have to make the forty-five-minute walk through the marsh to where the boat had let us off. Then we'd have to survive the trek again to return to the lodge. With two outings per day, this added up to three hours every day that would be spent slogging through the mud. The bright side of this was that I could count on a really good leg workout. The dark side was what my children might turn into, having to complete such feats. Ivy had been known to complain after walking a few feet on a paved surface; I couldn't imagine how these endless treks would go. On that first day, at least, both of my daughters proved up to the task. They'd long since given up on any attempt to stay clean, so they viewed the experience with excitement at the opportunity to again get muddy, rather than apprehension about the phys- ical challenges that lay before us. We reached the boat, and Sammy sat in the front while a guide who spoke no English sat in the back and took over maneuvering the boat.

"What's the other guide's name?" I asked Sammy.

"I'm not sure," he said. This amazed me, as the two seemed to know each other well, and it wasn't their first time working together. Knowing a fellow guide's name, I guessed, was far less important to Sammy than knowing the scope of the guide's abilities.

The ride was relaxing after the journey, and we puttered out to a larger confluence of the smaller tributaries, passing at one point what looked to be three houseboats grouped in an Amazonian neighborhood of sorts.

Sammy told us about the river dolphins, not all of which are pink, some are gray, and pointed them out to us as they surfaced on occasion near our boat. That both Emilia and Ivy were sufficiently excited upon seeing river dolphins relieved me. Popular culture has turned the word "dolphin" into something truly magical, and I worried that their expectations would be on that level. River dolphins will not flip in the air for you, talk to you, let you pet them, or appear to smile at you. They are a different lot with less endearing features, at least in terms of what we've been conditioned to think of as a dolphin. The word "pink" is used lightly to describe the male dolphins, and the pinkish parts are often mottled with gray.

"Some places on the Amazon let you swim with the river dolphins," Sammy said. "Don't do this. You are swimming with an animal that's caged every night. It's not a good thing to do. We don't offer that."

I was pleased to hear that, not only in the interest of preserving the animal, whose fate is not an optimistic one, but also because there was no way in hell I was inclined to jump into the brackish water that was home to many other creatures beyond river dolphins, including piranha, caiman, snakes, and fish that can burrow into your urethra as payback for peeing in their habitat.

We spent a good hour on the water, watching the dolphins, and as the sun began to sink made our way back to the getting-off point. As the boat gained speed, fish occasionally jumped around our boat, provoking nervous laughter as they did so. One fish jumped and, before landing *in* the boat, smacked my mother-in-law square in the chest. It was the harmless sort, no bloodthirsty piranha or urethra-seeker.

We passed the small neighborhood of three houseboats and watched as a boy, maybe three years of age, boarded a canoe from one houseboat and rowed to another, wearing nothing but his tighty whities. I thought of my daughters in their life jackets, how back in the States I won't let them walk to our neighborhood park unaccompanied, and I realized just how far from home we were.

"So, where are you from?" I asked Sammy as we puttered along. I suspected he wasn't Brazilian, and he spoke with an intriguing mix of accents.

"I'm from Guyana, but my parents were Indian," he said. "I came to Brazil to study the plants. There are so many remedies here in the Amazon, you wouldn't believe it. I'll tell you about them on the jungle walk tomorrow. Well . . ." he reconsidered, "I actually came here for the ganja, but what I'm most interested in now is learning about *all* of the medicinal plants."

At dinner that evening, we came to understand that the cooks at the jungle lodge were extremely talented. I'd thought that lunch had tasted so good because we'd been so hungry, but now I realized this was a truly phenomenal group of women preparing food for the camp. They worked incessantly, the kitchen always buzzing in preparation for the next meal. At times they worked without running water, using water from a five-gallon jug if needed, or by candlelight when the power was out. Not only did they continue without complaint and perhaps even joyfully, but the quality of the food never waned, even when the basic utilities did. One of the cooks, I noted, was the same woman who'd boarded the bus with her daughter on our journey. I looked around for the little girl but didn't see her.

After dinner that night, the power went out, and the camp continued on with the use of candles and flashlights. We resigned ourselves to the fact that there were still no towels or water, and we climbed into our hammocks. At the front of the hammock room was my mother-in-law, followed by my father-in-law and then Mike, Ivy, Emilia, and me. The seventh person staying in the hammock room on the other side of me was Marco, an Australian taking a Brazilian journey by himself. We settled in to go to sleep, and after twenty minutes, when the first of our numbers drifted off, the farting began. It was sporadic throughout the room; we'd all had beans at dinner. At one point, I almost fell asleep, but then my father-in-law got up to use the bathroom, and the process of getting in and out of the hammock, the flushing of the toilet, and the creaking of the floorboards under his feet kept me awake. I was silently annoyed, relieved when he returned to his hammock, and then further annoyed when I realized I too had to pee. The night was fitful, though the girls slept well. The last sound I remember before drifting off came from my mother-in-law. I can't speak to whether or not she was gassy, but I can attest to the fact that she is the only person I know who exudes so much joy that she laughs, heartily, in her sleep.

* * *

The Christmas Piranha

They're eating the guests, sir.

—*Piranha* (1995)

"Okay, who wants to see a tarantula?" Sammy asked. The North Face boys took a step back. The four of them were paired with the six of us for a jungle walk, led by Sammy, assisted by Ozéia, the guide who spoke no English but who'd piloted the small boat for our river dolphin cruise the night before. We'd learned his name by asking the kitchen staff, who were happy to provide little details like peoples' names, with which Sammy didn't bother.

We watched as Ozéia took a small stick and poked at a hole in the ground. I'd seen the same type of hole everywhere and hadn't given it much thought. But as I watched Ozéia prod a tarantula out of its den, I realized how thankful I was for the wooden walkway on which the jungle lodge existed, keeping us two feet off the ground while we ate, slept, and toileted.

As the tarantula emerged, Ozéia pinned it gently to the forest floor with the stick. Then Sammy picked it up, holding it for all to see and pointing out the creature's finer features.

I was nervous for what would happen when Ozéia released the tarantula, but it simply scurried back to its hole.

"Here we have some mosquito repellant," Sammy said. He motioned to an ants' nest attached to a tree. The size of a giant beach ball, the nest hung like a massive growth, and I wondered how many hundreds of thousands of ants comprised the colony. Sammy placed his hand on the nest, and we watched as a thousand ants swarmed up his arm. This time the entire group took a step back. When the ants covered him from fingertip to elbow, he used his other hand to crush them and rub them into his skin. "Here, smell." He held his arm up for all of us to lean in and get a whiff, as well as view the thousand bits of ant carcass that now coated his forearm. "Smells just like eucalyptus. Keeps the mosquitoes away." Then he batted suddenly at his arm again. "But if you don't crush them all, they bite you. That part hurts." I wondered what it must be like to have such tasks as a part of your daily job description.

Our jungle walk continued with the opportunity to swing on a jungle vine, about which the North Face boys were just as excited as my eight-year-old daughter. Both Sammy and Ozéia carried large machetes with them, used for hacking through dense growth and, on occasion, creating the perfect jungle vine from which to swing. They pointed out things we'd never have seen on our own, like a frog disguised as a leaf, and they used their machetes to make an endless string of gifts for Emilia and Ivy. From vines and palm fronds, they wove not only crowns and bracelets but a grasshopper and a fish on the end of a pole, like the Amazonian version of balloon animals. The jungle showcased the value of owning a large, sharp knife, not for protection from any threat but for making things. In idle moments, they whittled, carved, and braided all manner of objects.

We passed rubber trees and walking palm trees, their roots beginning high above the ground and seeking out new territory over time. "Here is a jungle cell phone," Sammy said, pausing in front of the giant, buttressed trunk of a great kapok tree. "If you are lost in the jungle, you find one of these, and you can use it to let people know where you are." He slammed the hilt of his machete into the trunk, and the sound reverberated.

They found Brazil nuts and hacked them open to offer to the group. Brazil nuts form inside of a capsule that resembles a coconut. When hacked open, it revealed a dozen or so nuts inside, their arrangement reminiscent of the segments of an orange. Everyone sampled the Brazil nuts.

"Here we have a different kind of nut," Sammy said. He cut a nut to expose a larva inside. "Anyone want to try? These grubs are edible. They don't taste bad." The four lawyers remained silent.

"Well, I'll try it," said Mike. I watched as my husband put the fat white grub in his mouth and chewed it thoughtfully. "Tastes like almond milk," he said. I silently vowed not to kiss him again until he'd brushed his teeth.

"Anyone else?" Sammy asked.

"Sure! Why not?" said my mother-in-law, before reaching for her own larva snack.

When our jungle walk concluded, we returned to camp. Drenched in sweat, I debated reapplying deodorant or attempting an actual shower. There was a trickle of cold water from the showerhead, and I used this and a sliver of soap to approximate bathing. There wasn't enough water to shampoo and rinse my hair, so I vowed to keep it in a bun and not contemplate its level of filth until we were back in civilization where I could do something about it. With no towel, I blotted myself with a dirty T-shirt and called it good.

We ate lunch and lazed on the deck outside of the dining hall. Sammy and some of the other guides continued with their jungle origami, presenting more gifts to the girls, including an approximation of a bow and arrow. Other guides offered them piranha teeth as souvenirs, the tiny, delicate jawbones kept safe in carrying cases fashioned from two caps from plastic bottles screwed together around the threads of a bottle neck. Sammy began a show of card tricks for Emilia and Ivy while I studied what Sammy had referred to as "fruit vultures" and the occasional toucan. Multicolored lizards skittered along the grass while monkeys, far more wary of our presence, kept their distance in the looming canopy.

"Sammy, is it possible for us to upgrade from the hammock room to one of the private cabins?" I asked. I shuddered at the thought of another long night in a hammock, listening to the gases and snores of half a dozen adults.

"I'm sorry," he said, "but we're totally full. I don't have any rooms open."

"That's fine," I said. "Just thought I'd ask."

Later in the afternoon, we set out to fish for piranha. This involved the same forty-five-minute trek through the mud that we'd done to reach the jungle lodge, and which we'd repeated in our quest to spy the river dolphins.

"Maybe we should try doing this barefoot," my father-in-law suggested.

"I don't know," said Nana.

"That makes me think of cut-up feet and flesh-eating diseases," I offered.

"It's how the locals do it," Mike said.

"I think it might be a lot easier than trying to maneuver in this muck with ten pounds of mud stuck to our shoes," Papa continued. "I think I'm going to find a big walking stick to have with me and give it a shot."

In the end, we all agreed to try it, even the children. I put flesh-eating diseases out of my mind and admitted we might be better served to learn from the local wisdom. After trying it once, we would adopt this technique for every trek through the mud.

There are different types of piranha, and the ones we caught were smaller and less aggressive than the type pictured in horror films, like the imaginatively titled *Piranha* of 1978. Piranha *fishing* first involves a fair amount of piranha *feeding*. The ravenous nature of the fish does not mean that they are careless creatures. The stealth with which a piranha can remove a cube of beef from a hook without you knowing is impressive. They are also more discerning than their reputation implies. They spurn meat that is too fatty or gristled. The fishing poles we used were not anything like a rod and reel but narrow sticks cut and carved, with a fishing line attached at one end and a simple hook. It is an elementary operation. After baiting a hook with a cube of preferably lean meat, you let the baited hook sink into the water, then thrash the tip of your pole briefly at the water's surface.

"You have to call the fish." Sammy demonstrated, creating a commotion with the end of his pole. "And then as soon as you feel a tug, you have to yank the line quickly to the side to snag them. Don't pull your line straight up or you'll hook someone in the boat." This instruction didn't prevent hooks from flying everywhere, and it's a wonder no one was seriously injured. The tight quarters of the small craft made it a relatively dangerous pursuit. Ozéia helped both Emilia and Ivy, despite a complete lack of English on his part and Portuguese on their part, though they did remember to say the occasional *obrigada* in thanks.

Time and time again, the piranha stealthily stole the bait without our knowledge, as we eventually lifted our hooks from the water to find the beef had been swiped. Over time, we improved, catching a few piranha and handing them directly over to Ozéia and Sammy to remove the hooks. Later we would grow braver and remove the fish from the hooks ourselves. Most of the fish were too small to keep, and we'd throw them back in, though half a dozen were substantial enough to serve as a future meal.

At dinner that evening (which didn't include our catch), I contemplated what could be used as earplugs as another night in the hammock room loomed before us. Sammy interrupted my thoughts.

"Okay, guys," he said, approaching a long picnic table in the dining hall where our group of six sat. "I have some rooms you can move to. Go get your stuff after dinner."

"Really?" I beamed.

"What do you mean we're going to move rooms?" Emilia said with a panic.

"Aren't we going to sleep in the hammock room again?" Ivy asked.

"We love the hammock room," Emilia said.

But I could tell from Mike's expression that he too was not looking forward to the hammock room again and that we would overrule our kids on this particular issue.

"There are rooms available now?" I asked.

"The four guys are leaving," Sammy said. And on cue, we saw the North Face lawyers, decked out in their thousand-dollar gear, gathering on the deck.

"I can't wait to get out of here," one said.

"I just want to be on a beach in Rio and have this all be a distant memory," said another.

One night had been enough for them, and they were canceling the rest of their Amazon trip and heading back to the city.

That evening, we moved into two rooms. My in-laws had their own bedroom and bathroom, and Mike and I shared the large bedroom, where two twin beds flanked a queen, with our daughters. We had a private bathroom as well, which, though less than sterile and still bug-infested, felt like luxury after the bathroom in the hammock room. We still had no towels but had long since resigned ourselves to drying off with dirty laundry, which there was no shortage of, as all of our clothes qualified.

After a glorious night's sleep on an almost-real bed, we woke to the thick, hot, jungle air and Christmas morning. We'd known in advance of the trip that we'd be in the jungle on Christmas, and Santa had graciously accommodated our travels by visiting us at our home in Boise a week before we'd departed for Brazil. Emilia and Ivy knew that the trip took the place of any gifts they might receive from us and so woke without any expectations of receiving presents. They were eager to give presents, however, as the 25th of December is my mother-in-law's birthday. When packing for the trip, they'd planned for the occasion with jewelry for their Nana, some purchased and some crafted.

"Come on, Mom and Dad! Let's go!" Emilia demanded.

Ivy was already out the door, leading the way to Nana and Papa's room. "When she opens the door," Ivy instructed, "we all sing 'Happy Birthday.'"

We did as we were told and presented Nana with her birthday gifts. My in-laws then presented each of us with a Christmas gift before we all walked to the dining hall for breakfast. We sipped coffee and chatted as Sammy approached.

"We'll be taking a trek to a local home," he explained, "so you can see a house and farm around here and how the people live."

"Do you think we should go barefoot again?" I asked. It had worked well while slogging through the mud, but I knew nothing about the terrain for which we were headed.

"I'm sure you know what's best," he said.

Well, no, I thought. *That's why I'm asking.* But Sammy seemed to think that motherhood bestowed upon me a wisdom not to be questioned. We decided to go barefoot.

The trek through the valley included the usual mud but then crossed onto tougher earth as we crested a hill to where a family lived. Sammy guided us along the grounds surrounding their house, pointing out the odd and alien-looking cashew trees, where cashew nuts (technically seeds) grow from under much larger cashew fruits and resemble something out of a Dr. Seuss book.

"These plants are called *lomboys,* and these are garlic leaves, and this plant is where the potato grows from a tree. This one is good for the prostate." All of the men perked up and paid attention. "This one is good for skin cancer. And this one is good for when you have too much weight on your shoulders." Sammy was a rapid-fire encyclopedia of natural remedies and salves. "Now we go see where they process the manioc."

"Mom," Ivy said with a quiver in her voice. "My feet hurt." The ground was no longer the soft, slick mud of the river basin, and the decision to walk barefoot proved to be a foolish one.

"Come here, Ivy," I said and crouched down so that she could get on my back. Mike did the same with Emilia.

Sammy led us to a small structure with rudimentary tools for the processing of manioc root into flour.

"First they're gonna use this thing here," said Sammy, "then they're gonna use this thing here, and then they're gonna use this thing here." He held up sieves, paddles, and unidentifiable tools in turn. His descriptions seemed lackadaisical when compared with the intricate knowledge he'd imparted just minutes before on various plants and their healing powers. "They make the *farinha*, the flour. They had flooding in 2009 and 2012, which raised the prices of the manioc flour. And this is how they make their living. They sell it to Manaus." His demeanor seemed subdued, almost dismissive. "But they have some of the poison in the manioc, and it makes them sick and stupid. They get the red eyes." He waved a hand at the tools. "You can use your imagination to think how it would work." I was surprised at his apparent disdain for manioc, the processing of it, and the people who make their livelihood from it, especially when I later learned that the house we visited belonged to Ozéia's parents.

Manioc is also known as cassava or tapioca, and certain varieties, improperly prepared, can result in cyanide poisoning, which was the danger of which Sammy spoke. If it's properly peeled, boiled, cut, and dried, the levels of cyanogenic glucosides are sufficiently diminished. And lord knows I hate it when my food has too many cyanogenic glucosides in it. It's a hearty, low-maintenance crop with high starch content, and as a result one of the leading food plants of the world and a major source of calories and carbohydrates in developing countries.

We got a brief glimpse of Ozéia's parents' home, where the presence of flat-screen televisions and other modern electronics seemed at odds with the nearby tributaries and jungle. Like Ozéia, his parents spoke only Portuguese, but his mother still successfully communicated how she felt about those of us who were barefoot. I gathered that she deemed us not very bright and noted that her toes were freshly and expertly manicured while mine were caked with filth.

As we trekked back down the hill, thankful to plunge our bare feet back into the squishy mud, which wasn't a sensation I'd ever anticipated being thankful for, we encouraged our children to walk.

"This hill is too steep, Ivy," I said. "You're going to have to walk yourself."

"But it's too steep for me to walk alone," she whined.

"You're just going to have to try," I said. "I can hold your hand, but I can't carry you."

A minute later, Ozéia swooped in and lifted Ivy, gracefully carrying her to the mud flats, where he set her on her own two feet. She reached to hold his hand for the rest of the walk back to the lodge. When we arrived, he took her to the hose and washed off her feet, which I knew solidified her crush on our strong, silent guide.

When we'd all cleaned up and sat on the edge of the decking before lunch, Ozéia used a large knife to clean the piranha we'd caught the day before. The girls and I watched at his side as he scraped the scales and scored the flesh.

"Oh no, a wasp," Emilia said, cringing from an insect hovering nearby.

Ozéia turned to look at why the girls were recoiling, not understanding their speech but sensing fear in their sudden change in body language. He paused in cleaning the fish, casually used his knife to spear the wasp against the counter, and flicked it into the grass before returning to the fish. After preparing the piranha, he fileted a few larger fish, discarding the innards in the direction of the nearby fruit vultures, who were all too eager to demonstrate that their diet wasn't limited to fruit.

Christmas lunch in the Amazon with a side of piranha felt oddly comfortable. Piranha is a delicate white fish, tasty, but with each fish providing only a tiny morsel of protein. We ate it as much for the novelty as to satiate hunger.

After lunch, the girls played hide and seek with Gabriella, the daughter of the cook we'd picked up on our way in. They formed a fast friendship through smiles and an innovative, instinctual sign language. Watching them play and giggle brought joy tempered by only a hint of sadness at the realization that our time in the jungle was finite. The people we encounter throughout the world enrich our lives, but the parting is often bittersweet.

* * *

Marco, Judy,
and Other Imaginary Friends

I don't remember anybody's name.
How do you think the "dahling" thing got started?

—Zsa Zsa Gabor

"**M**om, I have to go potty," Ivy said.

"I'll go with you," I offered, not wanting her to have to brave the facilities on her own.

"I have to go, too."

Ivy peed, then stood patiently watching me as I did the same. It's uncomfortable having a child stare at you while you sit on a toilet seat. In an effort to distract her, I said, "Ivy, look at that moth."

A pristine and beautiful white moth, with intricate designs decorating its wings, sat peacefully on the wall to my left. The creature perched in stunning contrast to the near-crumbling structure and the sea of filth and bugs that bathed it. Without a moment's hesitation, Ivy reached out a palm and slapped the moth.

"Ivy, why did you do that?" I asked. "It was so beautiful."

"I thought you said, 'Get that moth.'"

"No, I said, '*Look* at that moth.'"

"Oh," she said shamefully. "Sorry."

In her younger years, she'd been known to purposely step on a bug, then sheepishly look up and mutter, "Oops."

The moth didn't fall but seemed half-crushed and pasted to the wall in its own gore.

"Maybe it will, you know, feel better after it rests there for a bit," I said.

"Can we go to dinner now?" she asked. "I'm so hungry."

I looked at the carnage of the moth and its many cousins. "Yeah. Me, too."

At dinner that evening, Sammy announced, "Since it's Christmas, the staff will be preparing a second dinner tonight at midnight."

"There's no way," my father-in-law said. "I'm ready for bed now."

"Me, too," said Mike. "What time is it?"

"Seven o'clock," my mother-in-law answered.

We were all more than capable of staying up past midnight, but slogging through mud three hours of every day left us drained.

"You guys are all gonna come," Sammy insisted. "The kitchen girls are gonna make some big chickens, lots of food, a big cake. And we celebrate not just Christmas but also the birthday lady." He pointed a long finger at Nana.

My mother-in-law smiled. "Well, if we must, we must."

The girls napped in the evening hours, and we promised to wake them for the midnight party. As they slept, we passed the time at the lodge's tiny makeshift bar, where I stupidly ordered red wine. Brazil is not known for its wine, but beyond that, one should never order red wine in a tropical climate, where even the most sophisticated vintage will turn to vinegar in no time. We tried caipirinhas, though again, ice cubes were limited in such conditions, and the drinks served grew warmer and with less ice as the night wore on and depleted what ice they had. Beer was the best option.

At the midnight celebration, my mother-in-law was the guest of honor (after Jesus, of course), and the staff allowed Emilia and Ivy to decorate the cake they'd baked. My daughters, woken as promised after a few hours of sleep, slowly and with movements born of fatigue placed candied fruit on the frosted cake. We ate so as not to be rude, though everyone was still full from dinner and longing for bed. In the face of such hospitality, we sampled roasted chicken, half a dozen salads, and cake. The entire camp toasted my mother-in-law, raising glasses of unidentifiable fermentations. We shared laughter and food in the jungle as our numbers ebbed, with both lodgers and staff sneaking off when they could to find a few hours' respite before dawn. In the morning, the camp would wake groggily before churning to life and beginning the substantial cleanup of the orphaned beer cans littering every surface.

* * *

"Is Ramon still here?" my mother-in-law asked.

"Who's Ramon?"

"You know, the guy who lives in Australia. He was with us in the hammock room that first night."

"You mean Marco?"

"Oh, shit." My mother-in-law put a hand to her head. "His name is Marco?"

"That's okay," I assured her. "You called me Judy for the first week you knew me."

"I did, didn't I? I guess I thought you just looked like a Judy."

"Marco is actually packing up to leave now," I said. "We should say goodbye."

We walked to the top of the long staircase heading down, where Marco prepared to depart with a guide who would lead him back to Manaus.

"Hey, Marco," I called. "We just wanted to say goodbye."

"Oh." He smiled tentatively, and I wondered if there was something about me that he found off-putting. Maybe he was insecure about farting in the hammock room, like I'd been privy to a part of him I wasn't meant to know. Maybe I'd farted more than anyone else that night in the hammock room, and he simply found me disgusting.

"Write your name down, and I'll find you on Facebook sometime," I suggested.

"Okay." He took my journal from me and did so. "Have a good rest of your trip," he said. "It was nice to meet you all." We watched him begin the long journey back. I glanced at my notebook.

"Crap," I muttered.

"What is it?" my mother-in-law asked.

"His name is Michael. You've been calling him Ramon, and I've been calling him Marco. His name is Michael."

"Crap," she agreed.

"You'd think that would be the one name we could get right."

"At least I'm not the only one who screws up names," she said.

I later took my journal to Sammy. "Can you write down your mailing address so that I can send you something?" I asked.

"I don't read and write much, but you write down *your* e-mail, and I'll have my girl send my address to you."

"Oh. Okay." Had Sammy just given me a version of "Don't call me; I'll call you"?

"I never learned to read and write," he explained. "My parents sent me to the best schools, but it never took. It's the dyslexia."

"Okay," I said, not knowing how else to respond. Sammy spoke seven languages. I'd never been confronted with illiteracy in someone who spoke seven languages.

"Make sure your group gets good sleep tonight," Sammy said. "Tomorrow we're gonna do one last jungle walk in the morning with a new group of people. After lunch, a guide is gonna take you back to Manaus."

We followed Sammy's advice, and I woke the next morning to find Mike sitting up in bed, drinking coffee.

"Where'd you get the coffee?" I asked.

"I got up early and went to the camp kitchen." He passed me the small, porcelain mug. "I must not have latched the door all the way, and it drifted open. When I came back, the door was open, and you, Emilia, and Ivy were a little bit . . . exposed."

"Wow, thanks for that."

"It's okay," he said. "I'm pretty sure no one else was up and walking around."

"How reassuring."

We are not in the habit of family nudity, but the heat of the jungle and the scarcity of clean underwear (our swimsuit bottoms were a common substitute—we'd wash them in the sink at night when there was water and leave them to dry until morning) made nighttime nudity a common occurrence. Mike was the exception, always in boxers at the least, as he's less than eager to discuss male anatomy with his daughters.

The girls stirred and rubbed their eyes.

"What are we going to do today?" Emilia asked.

"We're doing another jungle walk," I answered.

"Oh, good," said Ivy. "Maybe that guy will wash my feet again."

After dressing in my least odorous shorts and tank top, I opened the door to enjoy the rest of my pilfered coffee on the tiny landing connecting our room to the wooden walkway that spidered through camp to keep us above ground and away from tarantulas. Two men stood on the landing of a room on the other side of the walkway, smoking cigarettes in their tight white underwear. At the sight of me, I thought they might show some discretion, but they appeared not to care and paid me no more attention than they did a nearby committee of vultures. For a moment, I feared they'd spied my girls and me sleeping in the buff through our open door and as a result decided that the lodge catered to nudists and the scantily clad. But their demeanor suggested instead that they just didn't care.

The smokers turned out to be part of the new group with whom we were paired for our jungle walk. Along with the men were their wives, an infant, and one sullen and overtly hostile teenage boy. They spoke Mandarin, which was not one of the seven languages in which Sammy was fluent, and depended on one of the wives to roughly translate. Our group quickly fell to the back, as the Chinese family walked on our heels, giving us the uncomfortable sensation of strangers breathing on our necks. I tried to remind myself that their behavior likely stemmed from simple cultural differences rather than blatant rudeness. The problem with walking in the back was that the two men and the sullen teenager smoked constantly, so our walk through the jungle left us moving in a cloud of second-hand smoke, and I died a little every time one of them flicked a cigarette butt into the Amazon jungle. It seemed an atrocity to nature. Tiny but atrocious nonetheless. One of the women carried her infant, and I marveled at her ability to breastfeed a child while walking through a rain forest and occasionally challenging terrain. This redeemed the group ever so slightly to me but only until the next cigarette butt was thrown.

The children began a slow melt. Having previously done the walk and with the heat and humidity at a wilting peak, their typical good nature and willingness to forge forth evaporated. Mike and I resorted to giving piggyback rides, which left us on the brink of our own physical breakdowns. Trudging through the jungle for forty minutes with a child on my back, with no clear idea of when our guide would lead us back to camp, created a dull ache in my biceps and irrational panic in my brain. If my body gave out and I died on the spot, would the girls have to travel with my corpse in one of the tiny boats along the tributary to get me back to Manaus? Such a trek would be too scarring for words, so I resolved to let Mike know to just bury me in the jungle and call it good. But I didn't drop, and Sammy mercifully brought the jungle walk to an end before I had a chance to discuss my wishes with my husband.

When it was time for us to leave the jungle lodge, Sammy presented me with a hair stick that he had carved from beautifully veined wood in contrasting black and white grain. "It's beautiful," I said. "Thank you so much." I knew it was better than any souvenir I would buy.

The girls said their farewells to Gabriella, Ozéia, and Sammy, and we showed our gratitude to our guides in thanks and tips they'd more than earned. Emilia and Ivy drew pictures and wrote thank-you notes. Sammy's illiteracy and Ozéia's lack of English made this difficult, so I read Sammy's cards to him, then read Ozéia's for Sammy to translate.

As we left the lodge, we heard other guests say that the boat was much closer than it had been in previous days, negating the forty-five-minute muddy trek. We looked down the hill to the winding tributary and saw a boat not far.

"Oh, wow. That's awesome," Nana said.

"Especially since this is the trek when we have to carry all of our stuff," I added, hoisting backpacks and bags.

"You mean we don't have to do the big walk?" Emilia asked.

"Nope." I smiled. "Just a short one."

We followed a guide, one of the many who spoke no English and appeared to be about fourteen years of age. But as he neared the boat, without slowing, and then walked past it without a glance, we realized our earlier information was little more than wishful thinking and gossip.

We made the full hike, arduous and muddy and loaded down with our backpacks, before reaching a small wooden boat with an outboard, which the young boy piloted. Our time on the water fostered an appreciation for the vessels in which we traveled. The boats were wooden, though too wide and flat-bottomed to be called canoes. Their outboards had been retrofitted with long shafts so that the propellers could be maneuvered well behind the boat and brought to just below (or even at) the water's surface. This allowed for propulsion of the boat through the shallowest of channels, critical during the time of year when we traveled the tributaries, when the heavy rains hadn't yet come to turn the dwindling streams into deep rivers.

After a forty-minute journey, we arrived at the same dock and store at which we'd stopped on our way out to the lodge. We drank beer and bought the girls juice while waiting for the van that would take us on our next leg of the trip back to Manaus. A couple from London was on their way out to the lodge, and we chatted, telling them what a great time we'd had and singing the praises of Sammy, Ozéia, and the phenomenal kitchen staff. As we spoke, I watched a wasp land on the woman's white tank top and begin making its way into her cleavage.

"Wasp!" I shrieked, but only *after* reaching for her, so for a moment it appeared that I was lunging for her breasts.

"Wow," said Mike. "So, that happened."

"I'm so sorry," I said to her. "I didn't mean to reach for your boobs."

"No, it's okay," she said. "I'd much rather that than have a wasp down there."

The van arrived, and we began the hour-long bumpy ride in the closed heat of the vehicle. We crossed miles of red earth before reaching a paved road, which led back to the small town where we boarded another boat, this one a "speed" boat when compared to the wooden watercrafts of the Amazon tributaries. We backtracked along the meeting of the waters before returning to Manaus to board yet another van. Eventually we were delivered to the tour office. The concrete sidewalks and glass windows and cars of the city seemed foreign after only a few days in the jungle without them.

Edison, who we'd met that first night in Manaus, manned the tour office still and greeted us warmly. "How was it, guys?"

"It was awesome," said Mike.

"My dad and Nana ate worms," Emilia added.

"I bet they were delicious," said Edison. "You ready for the boat tomorrow?"

We nodded. For our remaining three days in Manaus, we chartered a riverboat to take us to different portions of the Amazon.

"I booked you at a hotel just a few blocks away for tonight. I promise this one is much nicer than the one you stayed at that first night. I'll walk you over there." He did so and helped us check in, serving as translator between us and the desk clerk. "There's no charge for the kids," he explained.

"Okay, thanks so much," I said.

"Just come back to the tour office in the morning, and we'll get you to your boat."

Mike's parents headed to a room a few doors down from us.

Our room was miniscule and included one big bed, which clarified exactly why they'd been so generous in not charging additional fees for the presence of our children.

As we set down our things, I realized that my bag was partially open.

"Oh my gosh, Mike. I think our first aid kit was stolen."

"When?"

"Just now. On the walk here."

"You're kidding."

"No. I was pulling it behind me. Someone must have grabbed it when we were waiting to cross the street."

"Is that all that's gone?"

"Yes," I confirmed. "Someone out there is now well stocked in bandages and iodine."

"Well, let's make sure that from now on we keep our bags in front of us."

We desperately wanted to shower, but the hour was late, and we needed food, so we retrieved the in-laws, and the six of us walked to the plaza, dominated by the Amazonas Opera House, and sat at an outdoor table. We ordered fish balls, which I believe would have tasted better had they been given a more appealing name. Any type of protein served in ball or nugget form loses a certain amount of appeal. The adults drank caipiroskas (like caipirinhas but with vodka instead of cachaça, the liquor used in Brazil's national drink), and we all snacked on fries. Against all odds, we looked to our right to find we'd sat next to a German couple, two middle-aged men who we'd met at the lodge but who'd departed before us. They were headed to destinations throughout Brazil and were the first of many travelers we'd meet who'd embarked on months-long, worldwide journeys.

That night I had a glorious shower and washed my hair for the first time in six days. Our hotel room was nice but included tiny bugs crawling all over the sink, much like the miniscule ants that covered the kitchen counters at our exchanged home in Londrina. Our family of four did our best to sleep in the shared bed that night, with Ivy slapping me in the face only half a dozen times.

The next morning, we met Mike's parents in the lobby for breakfast before my mother-in-law and I left Mike and his father in charge of the kids while we went in search of an ATM. After the stealthy pickpocketing the night before, we felt like easy prey. Two foreign women on desolate streets in the early hours, searching for a place to procure cash. But we did so without incident, passing plenty of Sex Shops and Sexy Shops along the way. We spied an outdoor market from afar, and it beckoned to us, but there was little time. We had a boat to catch.

* * *

Nana Loses Her Shit

To him who is in fear everything rustles.

—Sophocles

"Why is that man just lying there?" Ivy asked as we made our way back to the tour office for the next leg of our adventure. The man in question was sleeping on the sidewalk, though in the eerie, half-dead sleep that some people manage to do with their eyes open. He looked deceased.

"Maybe he's homeless," I said. "Maybe he doesn't have anywhere else to sleep."

"Then why does he have clothes?"

"Being homeless doesn't mean being naked," I said, wondering why she thought the two were connected. How many naked homeless people had my daughter encountered at six years of age?

After checking in at the tour office, we stopped at a small market to buy alcohol, Band-Aids, and nail clippers. Alcohol was always on the shopping list, while the Band-Aids and nail clippers were purchased to replace the ones lost in our stolen first aid kit. From there we had a short drive, accompanied by Edison from the tour company, to a different port than the one from which we'd departed before. We boarded a double-decker boat and chatted with Edison while the captain and crew readied for departure.

"Your English is fantastic," I said. "Where are you from?"

"I actually grew up in the Amazon," he said. "I have thirteen siblings, and all but two of them moved away to Manaus or another city."

"How long have you been doing this?" Mike asked.

"Just a few years," he said. "Just while I'm working on my PhD in ornithology."

I'd assumed that Edison's tour guide job was a good gig for a kid who'd come to the city from the Amazon, and I chastised myself for the assumption that there wasn't more to him, as he was clearly far more educated and fluent than anyone in our group.

"You're kidding," I said. "Emilia would love to talk to you. She wants to be an ornithologist."

"Really?" His eyes brightened. "That's awesome. I study the harpy eagle. I've had a few expeditions searching out the nests. The harpy has two eggs, but when one hatches, the parents bury the second egg so that it doesn't hatch. So I wanted to create a program where we identify the nests, remove the second egg, and incubate it. But the program won't go anywhere, because I was told it would be interfering with nature." His shoulders slumped in disappointment and frustration. "And I said, 'What about deforestation? *That's* interfering with nature.'"

"Good point," I offered.

"My wife and I don't want to stay here anyway. She studies

nursing. We have a five-year-old and an eleven-year-old, and we're hoping to leave Brazil someday, find a place where we can have a better life. Maybe Australia."

We chatted a while longer, thanking him for all his help and wishing he was continuing on with us instead of heading back to the tour office.

"There's a different guide who will go with you on the boat," Edison explained. "His name is Geraldo."

On cue, Geraldo boarded the boat and introduced himself as Edison took his leave. Mike and I tried briefly to have a conversation with Geraldo and learn what interesting facts he might harbor. But Geraldo was much younger than Edison and hadn't yet found a calling or drive.

"I grew up in Manaus," he said. "It's a good job." He left it at that and didn't have much in the way of additional aspirations, though he was eager to do a good job as our guide and in the coming days would play countless games of Uno with Emilia and Ivy as the boat traveled from one destination to the next. Not everyone has patience for the torturous tedium of a game of Uno that will not end, and in that regard, Geraldo deserved full marks.

The boat set out, and we enjoyed the breeze that traveling on the water created. It was a welcome respite after the still and oppressive heat of the city. Traveling in a double-decker boat gave us a sense of security we hadn't realized was missing. When traveling in the small boats or walking through mud flats and jungle, we'd moved in close proximity to the tarantulas, piranha, and caiman that call the Amazon home. Now we had a buffer of sorts in the slow chugging of the vessel.

The lower deck of the boat included two bedrooms, one for Emilia and Ivy and the other for Mike and me. Both rooms had bunk beds, which delighted the girls, while Mike and I mentally prepared to cram together in the lower bunk in our room. Outside of these bedrooms was a main gathering area, underneath which lurked the ship's engine. A tiny kitchen off the gathering area was the size of a small pantry, yet miraculously home to all of the cookware and appliances needed to prepare meals for a party of nine. A small bathroom on the lower deck had a toilet, sink, a showerhead coming out of the wall, and a drain in the middle of the floor. It served our very basic needs but at the same time felt luxurious when compared with the amenities of the hammock room.

The upper deck had a large open area and the in-laws' bedroom, what would be considered the "master" bedroom and massive by comparison with the lower deck's sleeping quarters, with windows and a private bathroom en suite. Given that the ship's crew included our guide, Geraldo, the captain named Valzinho, and his wife, Jo, who would keep everyone well fed and the ship tidy, I wondered if there was a hidden row of bunks somewhere. It wouldn't be until the next morning, when I emerged for a trip to the bathroom, that I saw their hammocks strung across the space where we ate our meals.

Our first meal, however, would take place at a floating restaurant, where disembarking meant a harrowing walk across a narrow and questionable plank of wood. It's one thing for an adult to walk across such a thing and risk the embarrassment of a fall and dealing with soaked clothing. It's another thing to make such a trek with a six-year-old who can *kind of* swim. The security I'd felt from our substantial vessel dissipated. If one of our children fell in, I knew I'd jump in instantly after her, at which point my husband would have to save us both.

The restaurant offered an enormous buffet of beets and cardamom, roasted eggplant, fried eggplant, onion rings, salads, fruit, rice, beans, chicken, fish, and beef. It was a popular place to bring tourists like ourselves but also served the many Brazilians employed in various pursuits along the Rio Negro.

"Mom, can I go look at that stuff?" Emilia asked. One wall of the floating building was lined with narrow tables on which sat trinkets, art, and souvenirs for sale. These included horrific masks decorated with piranha teeth, so that the mouth of the mask included the tiny macabre jaws from the fish. I couldn't imagine why anyone would want such a thing.

"Those masks are totally creepy," I muttered to Mike.

"Look at these cool masks," my father-in-law said. "We might have to get one of these." I was sure he must be alone in this thinking, but then both his wife and Emilia emphatically agreed with him.

Before boarding the boat to continue along the river, we walked another narrow plank from the restaurant to the shore of a small island for a lesser version of one of Sammy's jungle walks, though it was quickly apparent that Geraldo had neither the knowledge nor the enthusiasm for the flora of the jungle that Sammy had. This fact, combined with the frequent litter along the path, didn't make us regret the present situation, but it did make us appreciate the experiences we'd had with Sammy and Ozéia.

"Mom, come in here," Ivy said. I joined her in the four-foot-wide hollowed trunk of a tree.

"This is kind of cool," I said. "It's like our own little secret hideaway."

"Look up," she commanded. I did so and realized that it wasn't as secret as I imagined, as two-dozen bats hung above us.

"I think that's kind of cool, and I'm also compelled to leave," I said.

"Bye, bats." She waved.

On our way back to the boat, we saw two obese children—or perhaps mother and daughter, it was difficult to tell—approaching us. Neither was taller than four feet. But it wasn't their obesity or stature that stole my attention. It was what clung to them. Each held a sloth. And as they approached us, it became apparent that this was their job, to keep sloths, find tourists, let the tourists hold the sloths, and get paid for it.

"Go ahead," Geraldo said. "You can hold them."

Sloths are wild animals that belong in the trees and that will in no way benefit from, and are likely harmed by, contact with humans slathered in sunscreen and bug repellant. The situation for these sloths was less than ideal. But all logic evaporated in the presence of such an animal. I reached my arms out, the handler placed the sloth on me, and the animal did the one thing that it knows how to do, which is hug. It was well groomed, appeared healthy, and had no odor of the kind that typically accompanies a wild being. And I clung to these things to justify my actions. I wanted to spend hours in that mutual hug, and I felt the sloth did, too.

I was sure it was smiling at me. I was sure it had nothing to do with the fact that the basic geometry of a sloth's face often makes it appear as if the animal is smiling. No, it was smiling at *me*. The girls each took a turn holding a sloth, as did my mother-in-law, who was shocked at how instantly the animal won her over.

Back on board as the boat cruised, we studied the land along the banks, passing slums and cargo ships, a middle-class stretch of shoreline, and then a section that boasted of wealth with beautiful beaches, resorts, and yachts. It was hazy on the river, with areas of water that were majestic in scope, while other areas held giant collections of litter. I spied beer cans, buckets, water bottles, plastic in every imaginable form, and then wondered what the river bottom must look like, as home to all of the litter that didn't stay afloat.

The perks of the boat, like running water and freedom from insects, were heavenly after the lodge, though I slept terribly on our first night aboard. Since Mike and I had our own room, separate from our daughters, I spent the night listening for them on the other side of our shared wall, fearful that someone would wake in the night and somehow fall overboard in a quest to find me. My paranoia reached a pitch when I contemplated forcing them to sleep while wearing life jackets or sleeping on the narrow floor space next to the girls' bunks in their room, so that they might step on me before venturing overboard.

* * *

"We're going to take a hike in the jungle," Geraldo said. "It's about a two-hour walk. We'll see some waterfalls. And then tonight we'll go looking for some caiman."

"That sounds great," I said, though fifteen minutes into the hike, Ivy turned to me and asked, "Mom, how many hours have we done of our two-hour walk?" Complaints aside, it was a jungle walk that was interesting but once again highlighted how lucky we'd been to embark on such experiences with Sammy and Ozéia.

We saw a kaleidoscope of butterflies along the trek to a small waterfall. Nearby sat a raised platform where backpackers sometimes slept in a makeshift camp, while others strung hammocks from tree branches both near to the ground and from dizzying heights. The sleepless night on the boat seemed distant and easily survivable by comparison.

Back on the boat, we traveled from the narrow tributaries of the Amazon to wide expanses where, had I not known otherwise, I'd have sworn we were on the ocean.

After dinner that night, our captain, Valzinho, readied a small boat that the larger vessel towed so that we might set out after dark in search of caiman. Valzinho piloted the craft, and Geraldo was tasked with grabbing the caiman for an up-close encounter with the crocodilians. We tooled around the waters and could see nothing other than the beams of light from Valzinho and Geraldo's flashlights. When one of the beams of light caught the glowing eyes of a lurking caiman, Valzinho slowly directed us closer. Geraldo leaned over the boat in a prime position to grab the reptile, then suddenly sat up in the boat and said, "Yeah, that one's too big."

"Well, we certainly don't want a big one to look at," said my mother-in-law.

Valzinho directed us to another one near the shore and expertly maneuvered the boat so that Geraldo could step onto land just feet away from a caiman.

"That one is too big, too," said Geraldo. The scenario repeated itself half a dozen times. Geraldo and Valzinho conversed. I didn't understand much of the Portuguese that passed between them, but it was apparent to all of us that this was not Geraldo's forte and that Valzinho was preparing to step in and show him how it was done.

Valzinho spotted a caiman, pulled the boat alongside the creature as it lurked in the water, and then exited the boat. He stood in his flip-flops and cut-off shorts, no protective rubber boots or thick gloves, in water up to his knees, unable to see anything other than where his flashlight shone.

"Oh dear lord," I said.

"He's either the coolest guy in the world or incredibly stupid," Mike whispered.

"Mom, I'm scared," said Ivy.

Valzinho handed his flashlight to Geraldo, who pointed them both at the caiman. In a flash of movement, Valzinho expertly grabbed the beast by its snout and tail as it thrashed around in protest. The caiman was three feet in length and therefore much larger than we'd anticipated. As soon as he plucked the reptile from the water and handed it to Geraldo, my mother-in-law began screaming.

"That motherfucker is not staying in the boat! Get that fucker out of here!" It should be noted that my mother-in-law is not generally considered a potty mouth. Nor is she inconsiderate of the delicate ears of my young children, but when confronted by the caiman, she lost all reason and perspective.

"Calm down, Mom," Mike encouraged. But the profanity continued for another thirty seconds until she realized that the animal no longer thrashed nor lunged for anyone's throat. It sat docile in Geraldo's lap while our guide used one hand to keep its jaws clamped shut and kept the other firmly on the reptile's body.

"Oh, Jesus," she muttered. "Oh, Jesus."

Valzinho repeated the process with an even larger caiman so that we might have the opportunity to study more than one species.

"So we can take these back to the houseboat so that you can have a better chance to see them in the light," Geraldo said. "But we'll need someone to hold one of these," Geraldo said, "so that Valzinho can drive us back."

"I'll hold one!" I volunteered, my hand shooting up in the air like an eager teacher's pet.

"We're taking them back to the boat?" my mother-in-law shrieked in horror.

"Yes," Geraldo confirmed. "That way you'll have a chance to take some pictures."

"I'll hold one!" I said again, louder this time to ensure that I was heard.

"So, we'll need one of you to hold one of the caiman," Geraldo repeated.

"I'll hold it!" I said again, and I felt like the kid in class who can't possibly raise her arm any higher, screaming at the teacher, "Pick me! Pick me!"

"I'll hold it," said my father-in-law quietly. Geraldo instantly turned to him and handed him the caiman. My feminist blood reached a steady boil from which it would not cool for at least the following hour. And I couldn't help but be reminded of the man standing at the airport with my husband's name on a card, despite the fact that I'd been the only point of contact in the preceding three months.

Back at the boat, we took the caiman into the dining area to learn about them, view them in better light, and take pictures. I grudgingly had a brief turn holding one, which was docile and resigned peacefully to being held at the jaw and tail by human hands. The other caiman was more agitated and thrashed about in the hands of my father-in-law, who had a slightly disconcerted look on his face, as if he was wondering what exactly would happen if he screwed up and the reptile broke free.

After subjecting the caiman to many photo ops, we let them go into the water, and I wondered with just a hint of melancholy if they would be able to find their way back home, to the banks from which we'd plucked them.

* * *

"Hey, Mom," Ivy said.

"Yes?"

We were soaking up the sunshine in plastic chairs on the upper deck. She stared down at the churning water behind us.

"If there was a sad old man on the boat who didn't want to live anymore," she said, "he could just fall off the back of the boat and not hold his breath."

"Wow, Ivy. I don't really know what to say to that."

"I think I have to go to the bathroom again."

"Um, me, too," I said. The rest of the day would unfortunately come to be known as Family Imodium Time.

Everyone had sufficient time with Imodium in their system before we visited the Tatuyo, a small tribal camp along the Rio Negro. The Tatuyo are accustomed to visiting tourists, for whom they demonstrate tribal dances and sell crafts and souvenirs. We sat in a large structure with a dirt floor and watched as the tribe danced, pausing in between each dance to explain the customs while Geraldo did his best to translate. The Tatuyo have their own language, but the chief did his best to explain in limited Portuguese. We learned that they grow manioc and ferment the root, supplement their diet with insects, and find excessive clothing unnecessary. Women refrain from covering their breasts, and children generally run about in underwear, though some wore traditional skirts and belts (for the benefit of us tourists, no doubt). I was a little apprehensive of how my children would react or what they might say, but they seemed unfazed or oblivious to the tribal customs of dress, despite that seeing a picture of such people in a book would inspire in them wonder and a steady stream of giggles.

"There were twenty-six tribes that came from the border of Brazil and Colombia," Geraldo translated. I wanted to know why they came, if they did so willingly, or if they were forcefully relocated. And did those twenty-six tribes still exist? "But this is the only tribe here," Geraldo continued, "and they do shows every day for the tourists. He says that part of their customs involve a three-day ceremony when it's time to pick the next chief." The chief continued speaking for another full minute, and I craved the reveal of more information, but Geraldo only looked at us with a sheepish grin and said, "And I'm not sure what that last part he said was."

After the partial translation, we were invited to walk the grounds of the small settlement and take pictures with tribal members. We saw blue macaws, a green parrot, chickens, dogs, and an inexplicable lone white rabbit. With time to spare, we wandered back into the large structure and browsed through the crafts for sale. Mike and I agreed to let each of the girls pick something as a souvenir.

"Oh, how about this?" Emilia said, approaching a large dart gun.

"How about a necklace?" I suggested.

"Or this!" She pointed to a giant headdress.

"How would we ever get that home?" Mike reasoned.

"I'll just wear it on the plane."

"I don't think that's going to work," I said.

"Okay, I've made my final decision." She quietly walked to a bow and set of arrows. The bow was about a foot taller than she was.

"I'm just not sure that's going to travel well," I said.

Eventually we convinced her to go for a large flute, which, though couched delicately in T-shirts inside of my suitcase for the rest of the trip, would refuse to ever produce a single note after arriving on American soil.

"I'll choose this," Ivy said, coming at me with what appeared to be a dagger. On closer inspection, I saw that it was a hair stick, at the end of which were tied bright yellow feathers.

"That will look pretty in your hair," Emilia said.

"And if you're ever attacked, you have a weapon at the ready," I added.

Mike bought me a hair stick as well. It was a twig when compared to the intricate one Sammy had made for me, and capped off with what appeared to be a large dried fish scale. It wasn't something I would have picked out on my own, but Mike felt compelled to purchase it after knocking over half of the items on that particular vendor's table.

We migrated to a corner of the structure where a large bowl of cooked ants sat, available for visitors to sample. At least I assumed they were cooked, but I'm not very good at eyeballing the "doneness" of a bowl of ants. They weren't moving, and I could only assume that this was the result of being cooked. My father-in-law pinched a few of them between his fingers and threw them back into his mouth as if they were peanuts. He looked thoughtful for a moment, said, "Huh, not bad," and then went back for seconds. Next to the bowl was a makeshift grill with a few unidentified, charred items on it and one unmistakable caiman tail.

* * *

Every Dog Has His Apron Dress

Dogs don't rationalize. They don't hold anything against a person.

—Cesar Millan

"We should dock in about forty-five minutes," Geraldo said. "And the van will meet us, take you to the ATM and the tour office, and then straight to the airport." Because of Brazil's restrictions on withdrawing substantial amount of funds, we still owed a chunk of cash to the tour company.

"Sounds good," I said. "I think we're just about packed." I went to the room where Mike and I slept to find him zipping up his backpack.

"Guess what I just found," he said.

"An orphaned baby sloth who wants me to be her new mommy?"

"No. But I did find our 'stolen' first aid kit."

"You're kidding!"

"It was at the bottom of my bag the whole time."

"Oh man. We are such assholes," I said. We'd fallen victim to paranoia. When you travel to places where people feel compelled to tell you about all of the crime that occurs there and all of the bad things that could happen to you, you find yourself at risk of instantly assuming that every misplaced item has been stolen from you.

"Why are we stopped?" Mike asked.

I realized that the boat was very quiet.

"I don't know." We walked to the main deck to find the floor opened up and Valzinho working in the depths of the boat's engine. "Well, that's not good," I said. We spent the next fifteen minutes drifting and wondering if we'd make our plane. I was compelled during that time to try to consume all of the remaining beer, as we wouldn't be able to take it with us. I didn't want to be wasteful.

"Are we going to get back in time?" my mother-in-law asked Geraldo.

"Yeah, I'm sure it will be fine," said Geraldo. "We might have to call another boat to come get you." These two statements contradicted one another. Was it going to be fine or did we need to be rescued?

"I don't think we're going to make our flight," said Mike.

"It's not looking good," agreed his father.

After twenty more minutes of feeling helpless and agreeing that we probably wouldn't make our flight, Valzinho emerged from the hold, drenched in sweat, and we were back on track as if there'd never been cause for worry. At the dock, we bade Geraldo and the crew farewell and hurriedly boarded the van that would take us to the cash machine, tour office, and airport.

The van's driver was aware of the time crunch. The guiding principle for navigating a vehicle in Brazil might best be described as willy-nilly. Drivers create lanes where there are none, and the degree to which they heed traffic lights and signs corresponds to how badly they want to get where they're going. As such, our driver handled the van like a NASCAR driver in contention for . . . whatever it is NASCAR drivers hope to win. He drove in lanes of oncoming traffic and snaked the hulking van through impossibly narrow gaps.

I silently willed him to slow down just as Mike leaned over and whispered, "This guy is amazing."

"I hope we make the plane," my father-in-law said.

"We're almost there," I whispered to my mother-in-law. "Because I remember it was really close to that Sexy Shop."

"You're right," she agreed. The van pulled up right in front of the Sexy Shop while my mother-in-law and I ran to the ATM for cash to pay our balance due.

When we returned, Mike whispered, "I just spent the last five minutes trying to occupy our kids so they wouldn't ask questions about the Sex Shop."

"Dad of the year," I said.

Edison was working in the tour office, and we thanked him for everything and wished him well. The driver whisked us off to the airport, where we stood in a long line for a few minutes before someone waved our group of six to the priority line.

"Well, that was convenient," my mother-in-law said.

"Did we get priority because of the kids or because you guys are old?" I asked, remembering the previous attendant who'd given them priority because of their age.

"I don't know," she said, "but I'll take it either way."

We boarded on time, and Mike sat with the girls in a bank of three seats, while I took the seat across the aisle. My husband would much rather be the parent on duty than risk sitting next to a stranger. The two seats next to me remained empty.

"I wonder who it's going to be," I said to Mike, motioning to my absent seatmates.

"Maybe no one." He smiled.

"I don't dare to dream," I answered. It was good that I didn't get my hopes up, because a couple then boarded. The man looked completely normal, until I noticed that he carried a purse with a dog in it. He sat next to the window. His wife followed and took the middle seat. She wore golden, five-inch heels accented with rhinestones. She was perfectly manicured and dressed to the nines. I hadn't showered in days. Her pedicure was immaculate with decorative flowers. My toenails were yellow, and I was pretty sure that I smelled bad. She took the dog from its carrier, and the couple spent five awkward minutes putting an apron dress on the dog. They took a selfie with the dog. Then they spent another awkward five minutes taking the dress off the dog. A flight attendant approached and held a Styrofoam cup of water for the dog while it drank, lest it begin the flight feeling parched.

As the plane took off, I directed my gaze across the aisle at Mike and the girls. The couple and their dog seemed like a decadent and pristine display of wealth and high fashion. I had to turn away. I wanted to remember every moment of the Amazon, to relive the time we'd spent with Sammy and Ozeia and the Tatuyo tribe. I wasn't ready to replace those interactions with images of expensive jewelry and tiny dogs carried around in purses and dressed in various outfits. Eventually curiosity got the better of me, and I glanced over to see the wife using her perfectly manicured hands to hit the dog on the top of the head. I wondered what its transgression was. Maybe the woman, with the dog on her lap, realized that giving her miniscule pet a large quantity of water to drink hadn't been a great idea.

* * *

It was well after dark when we arrived in Rio de Janeiro. We grabbed a cab from the airport and gave the driver the address of an apartment we'd booked online. Without any further guides or translators, I was back in the role of main communicator for our group, constantly trying to add new Portuguese phrases to my limited repertoire.

When we were dumped on the sidewalk outside of the building with our mountain of backpacks, there was no one there to meet us and the apartment building was locked. I felt like bait. Three generations of Americans standing on a dark street in Rio at night. The situation was less than ideal.

When the woman who owned and rented the apartment eventually showed up, I breathed a sigh of relief. We had to go upstairs in shifts on a tiny elevator to a bare-bones apartment. What appeared to be beds were thin pads on plywood. The heat was stifling. After so much time spent in the Amazon, we were all eager to shower, but just as in the jungle lodge, there were no towels. But there was a washing machine, and we'd all long since run out of any clothing that could be described as clean. Including underwear.

My father-in-law and I peered into the tiny kitchen. "Well, I don't think anyone will be doing any cooking in here," I said.

"Probably not," he agreed.

Then I remembered all of the incredible meals that Jo had prepared in the miniscule boat kitchen for the passengers and crew. And given our recent experiences, even the presence of a fridge was appreciated. We showered, washed clothes, and dried them on a rack that lowered by pulley from the kitchen ceiling, which is the sort of clever accommodation you find in tiny apartments.

The next morning, we set out to get the lay of the land, and it quickly became clear why Mike had booked the apartment. It was located just two blocks from Copacabana Beach, with plenty of shops and restaurants nearby. Rio had a vibe, a pulse to it. It was a place of music and thongs, cocktails and vendors, and seemed the antithesis of the jungle where we'd been only twenty-four hours before. We had no idea just how much the vibe of Rio would intensify in the twenty-four hours to come.

* * *

Christh the Reminder

Rio de Janeiro—A city where poverty, indulgence, crime, celebration,
beauty, passion and future all live in strange harmony.

—TheCounterIntuitive.com

We typically work every day when we travel, but the Amazon jungle had been a weeklong exception, during which we abandoned any attempt to maintain contact with the world back home. Rivers, jungles, and smothering humidity are not good companions for electronics, in any case. So, on New Year's Eve morning in Rio, Mike's parents agreed to take Emilia and Ivy to the beach early in the day so that we might get caught up on work. We plugged in to answer e-mails, check banking, and assure ourselves that we hadn't suffered any professional catastrophes during our week off the grid. After a few hours, we walked to the beach to meet up with Nana, Papa, Emilia, and Ivy.

Copacabana is a fairly wide beach from the sidewalk to the water's edge, so it's a bit of a walk across the hot sand to the prime real estate for beach lounging. To save everyone's feet, hoses are stretched out with periodic holes in them. This creates pathways of wet sand for people to walk on. As Mike and I did so, heading toward the area where we'd agreed to meet up with Mike's parents and our children, we passed a woman, perhaps seventy years of age. She stood stock-still and facing the sun, either zoning out or worshipping a sun god, with her swimsuit straps pushed down on her shoulders in an attempt to thwart tan lines. She didn't move or blink, and had she not been upright, I might have thought her dead.

"Should we do something?" I asked Mike, nodding in her direction.

"Like what?"

"I don't know. I feel like someone should bring her a chair or something."

I've people-watched on many beaches. I've seen sunbathers of all kinds. But I'd never encountered someone who felt the need to stand and face the sun, as if her posture might garner her more vitamin D than other beachgoers.

It's fairly easy to spend all day at Copacabana Beach. You can inexpensively rent chairs and umbrellas, and there are plenty of vendors to keep you fed, quenched, and entertained. You can purchase beach toys, sunglasses, caipirinhas, beer, cashews, water, sarongs, swimsuits, and sodas. I was eager to try the charred cheese on a stick and was amazed by the operation. The cheese vendors walk around carrying little ovens filled with hot coals. This often takes place on an already hot beach. When they have a customer, they take a skewer with a long rectangle of deliciously mild cheese on it, stoke the coals, and char the cheese to perfection. I was almost tempted to try the shrimp skewers, until I remembered that they sell and consume the shrimp with the shells on in Brazil. I wasn't ready for that. The caipirinhas came in a variety of flavors. I was partial to the classic lime but also a fan of the passion fruit. One vendor walked around with a yoke over his shoulders and steel kegs at his waist on either side.

"Excuse me," I said in Portuguese. "What is that?"

He answered, but I couldn't decipher what he was saying, so he took a cup and gave me a sample. On one side was tea and on the other a sweetened, lemonade-like drink. Because I'd stopped him and received a free sample, I felt compelled to buy a cup, but when I returned to the group, they saw the look of disappointment on my face.

"What is it?" my father-in-law asked.

"It's sort of like a sweet tea." I passed the cup around so that everyone could have a sample.

"You were hoping it was something with alcohol, weren't you?" my husband asked.

"Well, yes. Yes, I was," I conceded.

"Let's check out these sarongs," Nana said, flagging down a passing vendor.

The sarongs were beautiful and, like everything in Brazil, inexpensive when compared with American goods. My mother-in-law and I perused them while Mike played with the girls in the surf.

"What do you think of this one?" I asked. It was an elegant pattern in black and green, dominated by an elephant.

"It really accentuates your ass nicely," my mother-in-law said, which I mentally added to the long list of things I never thought I'd hear from my mother-in-law.

"You have an elephant ass," my father-in-law said.

"Excuse me?" I gaped at him.

"I mean, that's a good thing," he stuttered. "I mean, it looks good on you."

"Honey," my mother-in-law interjected. "You are digging yourself a hole."

"I'll forgive the elephant ass comment," I said. "You can buy the next round of caipirinhas." My father-in-law nodded in agreement.

The tradition on New Year's in Brazil is to wear white, so after the sarongs, we stopped a passing vendor selling beach dresses. He had white ones, and I asked to try them on. The first dress I put on brought with it the possibility of getting awkwardly trapped in an article of clothing in front of a large crowd of people. When I realized the dress was too small, it was too late, as I had one arm and half of my head sticking up out of the dress, and the fabric stretched tight across my chest, mashing my breasts as if they were bound with duct tape. In addition to the embarrassment of being temporarily trapped in an article of clothing, I also had the fear that I might rip the dress in my efforts to either get it all the way on or remove myself from it.

"Oh dear," my mother-in-law said. "Do you need help?"

"Nope," I said in my most casual, I-do-this-every-day-and-there's-nothing-at-all-the-matter voice. "But I think this one might be a little snug." Everyone knew this was a gross understatement, but they spared me the humiliation of pointing it out. I removed the dress and handed it to my mother-in-law, who wore it well.

I asked the vendor if he had a larger version, which he did and which didn't threaten to strangle me, so my mother-in-law and I ended up with matching white beach dresses.

When Mike and the girls returned to our spot for a break, the adults chatted about what else we might do in Rio, agreeing that after our time in the Amazon, we were all exhausted and probably content with just enjoying the beach.

"I'm still not feeling 100 percent anyway," said Mike. I'd likely passed my initial sickness after arriving in Brazil on to my husband, and he'd been periodically feverish and achy in the preceding two weeks, alleviated somewhat by antibiotics we'd procured from a travel doctor before the trip.

"Do we want to go see Christ the Reminder?" my mother-in-law asked.

"Christ the Redeemer," I corrected.

"Well, if we see Christ the Remainder," Mike said, "it will have to be tomorrow."

"Christ the Redeemer," I said again.

It is impossible for me to be any less religious than I am. Religion and I have simply never gotten along. That said, part of me wanted to see Christ the Redeemer/Reminder/Remainder, just for the chance to lay eyes on a statue of such scale. There's something undeniably impressive about an almost-hundred-foot statue built almost one hundred years ago.

For the time being, we contented ourselves with the phenomenal people-watching on Copacabana Beach. I was a little apprehensive about spending a day with so many buttocks in view. Would my husband be tempted by so many bronzed Brazilian asses? Would it heighten my insecurities about my body? But the beach has the opposite effect, because the thongs on Copacabana Beach are not reserved for young, tight bodies. Old and obese women wear thongs, too. Men wear Speedos or board shorts. The general feeling is that everyone lets everything hang out. After the initial shock, it ceases to carry any weight or importance. And after an hour, *not* wearing a skimpier cut of bathing suit starts to feel conspicuous. My daughters seemed oblivious to the different bodies and levels of dress, which is how it should be. It just isn't as important as we somehow make it out to be.

We spent the day drinking, laughing, playing with the girls, and watching groups of boys play with soccer balls, displaying a shocking level of talent and agility, so common in countries where soccer is sacred.

As evening approached, we walked to the promenade of restaurants separating beach from city and ordered pastels at a corner shop. These are a favorite Brazilian fast food, rectangles of fried dough with a variety of fillings. I ordered a few cheese pastels for myself and the girls.

"What do you want?" I asked Mike. "One with chicken?"

"I think I'm going to order the cheeseburger," he said.

"You're in Brazil and you're going to order a cheeseburger?"

"What? You don't think that's a smart move?"

"I don't know. I just figured you'd want something more . . . Brazilian."

"I'm going for the cheeseburger."

Twenty minutes later, I was feeling the unhealthy glow of someone who's just consumed fried dough and cheese. I thought next time maybe I'd follow Mike's lead, but then he turned to me and said, "Don't order the cheeseburger."

To maintain your sanity and your personal space on New Year's Eve on Copacabana Beach, you use candles. Mike bought these from a vendor and set them up in a circle in the sand, denoting our claimed spot. Inside the circle of candles, we arranged our chairs in a half circle, and these cradled a patch of sand on which the girls napped, sarongs both under them and over them. They'd drifted off with the promise that we'd wake them in time for the fireworks show. Only at one point in the evening did a drunken man come close to crossing through our circle and stepping on our children, who resembled nothing more than a pile of beach towels in the dark, but I quickly bodychecked him.

My daughters' ability to nap on noisy beaches has come in handy on more than one occasion. It allows them to make it through situations that people wouldn't normally consider kid-friendly, like spending fourteen hours on Copacabana Beach on New Year's Eve, culminating in the midnight fireworks show.

I've always found the hours between ten and midnight on New Year's Eve the most difficult. These are hours when I'm normally asleep, and staying up is extra painful when I see my girls sleeping and just want to cuddle up next to them. That said, Copacabana Beach was too eventful to consider sleep. Bands rocked on periodic stages set up along the beach. Revelers set bouquets adrift in the water. I was thankful Emilia and Ivy slept, as when they'd been awake they'd made a game of collecting the bouquets that drifted back to shore, which likely was not what the people launching the offerings had intended.

These were also the hours during which Mike, his parents, and I stopped drinking. We'd nursed drinks throughout the day, but we all held apprehension about how rowdy and crowded the situation would get with two million people on a beach, and we wanted to have our wits about us.

As promised, we woke the girls just before midnight for the most impressive fireworks display I'd ever seen. It was about twenty minutes long and launched from barges hovering off the coast. A pathetic fireworks show is depressing, especially when you've struggled to stay up well past your bedtime for it. Rio didn't disappoint, and there's a reason why the city is known for having the most popular New Year's

Eve celebration in Brazil, on a scale that has come to rival the festivities of Carnival.

The fact that the evening was such a success made me contemplate whether I'd ever consider celebrating the new year in Times Square. I thought not, given that there would be no soft patch of sand on which the girls could nap, as well as the fact that we're often less tempted by festivities in our home country. While we'd welcomed the opportunities to celebrate the new year on Rio's famed Copacabana Beach and also looked forward to experiencing Carnival in São Paulo, the Brazilian family with whom we'd swapped homes seemed shocked that we'd want to do these things, especially with kids in tow. There's also the inclination to put off seeing the sights of your own country because you feel like you can do so at any time, but traveling to another country makes such things seem like once-in-a-lifetime opportunities, which motivates you to take advantage of the experiences.

I felt that celebrating New Year's in Rio was a good *once*-in-a-lifetime experience and decided I was comfortable checking it off my list, just as my mother-in-law offered her take on the event.

"Wow," she said, "I *definitely* want to do that again, at least once more in my lifetime."

When the fireworks ended, we faced the daunting task of exiting the beach and making it back to our crappy apartment without getting separated or losing anything or anyone. It was a mass exodus, and when one man pushing through the crowd threatened to separate me from my daughters, I sharply yelled at him in Portuguese.

At twelve thirty we found ourselves back "home." Despite the late hour, I hopped in the shower and made the girls join me in an attempt to remove sand from them before putting them to bed. We dried ourselves with sandy sarongs, which somewhat defeated the purpose, but it was better than nothing.

Instead of visiting Christ the Redeemer/Reminder/Remainder, we spent New Year's Day recreating New Year's Eve in a gluttonous display of sloth while lounging on the beach. Copacabana was crowded, and at one point a young man sat by himself a few feet in front of our group. He had shorts, a hat, a T-shirt, and nothing more. When he took off his shirt, I noticed a large abrasion on his left shoulder. Pink, raw skin stood out, the type of wound I associate with road rash and a motorcycle ride gone wrong. He looked sixteen. After a few minutes in the hot sun, without the comforts of the chairs and umbrellas with which we lounged, he placed his hat neatly on top of his T-shirt and went into the water, wading in until knee deep, then diving forward into an oncoming wave. I watched him swim, tread water, and watch the people around him. He made no effort to interact with anyone, though every now and then he glanced back at his shirt and hat to make sure they remained undisturbed where he'd left them.

A vendor walked by, and we ordered another round of drinks as well as two bags of some sort of Brazilian snack, a crisp of sorts, like cheese puffs without any flavoring. We all sampled them before agreeing that no one liked or wanted them. They would later be discarded.

The teenager continued to bob in the water and eventually returned to his patch of sand, where he sat and stared at the sea. After another fifteen minutes, he repeated the process, entering the water to cool off, or pee, or maybe both. He could not have been in possession of a wallet or anything else, as he submerged himself fully in the water and each time left only his T-shirt and hat on the beach. No wallet, no phone, no water bottle or keys. Nothing. After watching him for an hour, wondering if he had a home, wondering how he'd procured his injuries, studying what appeared to be a slight and malnourished frame, I was reminded that while Brazil is home to famed beaches and festivals, it is also a country of poverty and corruption that perpetuates that poverty. That isn't to say that corruption perpetuating poverty is a problem unique to Brazil, though I'd go so far as to say it's undisputed there.

Our excess, of drink and food, our willingness to purchase half a dozen sarongs on a whim, all of these things held us in stark contrast to the reality of the boy before us, who eventually moved away when Ivy's playing in the sand threatened to encroach upon his tiny allotment of space. I wrangled her back, but the teenager moved on.

The majority of Brazilians on Copacabana Beach enjoy a different walk of life. Many pride themselves on their beachwear, and it's quickly apparent why waxing of a certain manner is called "Brazilian." For a decade prior to our trip to Brazil, I'd had monthly waxes of my nether regions. I ceased this practice after I could no longer ignore the ridiculous nature of the act. Paying someone money to smear you with hot wax before painfully ripping it off, along with your natural hair, in the hopes of attaining some sort of aesthetic, is illogical at best. But of all the times in my life to stop engaging in monthly Brazilians, it's ironic that I stopped doing so right before traveling to Brazil. Having returned my body to a more . . . *natural* state was good, as it kept my husband from ever encouraging me to wear a string in my ass and call it a bathing suit. Even love has its limits.

* * *

Flight of the Opossum

*A journey is like marriage. The certain way to be wrong
is to think you control it.*

—John Steinbeck

"So you know we have the Olympics coming up here in Rio," said Jennifer, an Australian tour guide working in Brazil. "Many of the athletes are already here and training. And do you smell that smell?" She waited for a second as we inhaled a pungent stench and scrunched our faces as if willing our nostrils to retreat from the odor. "Yeah, that. It wasn't until the athletes started to get sick that they realized there was sewage in some of the water they'd been swimming in. But that's Brazil for you."

I shifted my weight in my seat, as if that would somehow create more space. My mother-in-law sat to my right, a young Canadian couple sat to my left, and behind us were three more rows of seats with the rest of my family, a group of touring Australians, and a Chilean family. In the front row sat Jennifer, flanked by the driver and another tour guide named Manoe (pronounced Mah-NOO) from the Netherlands. Manoe turned around in her seat and addressed me.

"It's just these first two days that we're all together," Manoe explained, motioning to the passengers sardined in the van. "And then I will travel on with your group, and the others go on a different tour."

"Where are we headed now?" my mother-in-law asked.

"It's about a three-hour drive to Arraial do Cabo," Manoe answered, and we nodded as if knowledgeable on the coastal hotspots.

It was day one of an eleven-day journey along the coast from Rio to Salvador. We'd opted for a guided tour that promised to get us off the beaten path. The three-hour drive, due to the popular destination and single narrow road, took six hours in total. This was the first of many such miscalculations on the tour. We'd soon learn that for any estimated time of arrival given, we could add two hours at best and double it at worst. As the hours dragged on in the cramped space of the van, I wondered what could possibly be worth such a trek.

When we finally reached Arraial do Cabo, known for stunning beaches and as the best diving spot in the state of Rio de Janeiro, getting out of the van felt like heaven. We had an hour to ourselves before a scheduled cruise, and our group of six broke away from the others and descended on an outdoor table at a small restaurant for lunch. I left the other adults to order while I took the girls to an almost tolerable bathroom and then bought them each an açaí smoothie at a nearby smoothie stand. They'd endured six painful hours in the van, which had been enough to bring the adults to tears, and I wanted to reward them for it. Açaí smoothies are apparently healthy, which is hard to believe after you consume mass quantities of this frozen dessert. The berries themselves are rich in antioxidants (I don't actually know what that means, but I know the phrase is tossed around as a good thing), and Brazilians have been eating açaí forever, but we Americans have of course done our best in recent years to weigh in as major contenders when it comes to açaí consumption.

"What did you guys order?" I asked when the girls and I returned to the restaurant.

"Calamari, chicken, and french fries," my husband answered. I pictured the fried array of food to come and realized that the "treat" the girls were consuming would be the healthiest thing they'd eat all day. When the chicken arrived, it came atop an enormous bed of fries. Then the calamari came. And then a third platter with another mountain of fries. We hadn't yet learned that most things in Brazil came with french fries, and additional orders are unnecessary. We finished what we could, leaving heaping plates of food behind, and hurried to the marina to meet up with the rest of the group.

We were to embark on a three-hour cruise to three of Arraial's famous beaches. We reconnected with Manoe and the Canadians, with whom I felt a strong bond, having been smashed against them in the van for six hours, and then proceeded to wait for two hours in the stifling heat.

Brazilian heat was nothing new to us, but it intensified in the area in which we waited. A large paved gathering area bordered the massive docks, which served an endless wave of booze cruise boats dropping off partiers and picking up new batches. We felt like cattle in a crowded pen, and the masses of tourists around us dashed our hopes of experiencing something off the beaten path. The major attraction of an area is not necessarily the best place to be. Our confidence in the tour and excitement for the next week and a half began to waver.

It's one thing to wait for two hours in oppressive heat but another matter to do so with children. They'd walked for two hours in such heat in the Amazon jungle, but with constant points of interest in front of them. Standing on pavement in a crowd for two hours is far more difficult.

With nothing to occupy ourselves and growing doubts that we would ever be able to board a boat, we abandoned the group in favor of a few small shops on the other side of the square.

"Oh, look!" Ivy said at a store of random knickknacks, souvenirs, and beach gear. She pointed to a child's bathing suit, a one-piece (not terribly common in Brazil) with a picture of Elsa from Disney's *Frozen* on the front. I have a love-hate relationship with *Frozen*. On the one hand, it was a fairly cute movie, but Disney's insertion of Elsa's entirely unnecessary booty shake, combined with the incessant playing of "Let It Go" for an interminable amount of time after the movie's release hovered right around irksome. I frowned but thought logically about it. Ivy had been wearing a rotation of hand-me-down bathing suits that had gone through two cousins and her sister before becoming hers. This meant that the suits were worn thin, the fabric pilled in spots, and all of them had laughably saggy butts, so that Ivy appeared to have a load of sand (or worse) in her suit whenever she donned one of them.

"I don't want to buy her a *Frozen* bathing suit," Mike said.

"But she really needs one. Think about the bathing suits she has now."

He took a moment to picture the saggy-ass look that our six-year-old sported whenever we were at a beach and shrugged. "Whatever you want to do."

Because of the strength of the dollar and weakness of the real, everything in Brazil seemed cheap, and I defaulted to making the purchase whenever in doubt. Ivy's butt would sag no more.

"Thank you so much," Ivy said. "I love it so much I want to sleep with it." She cuddled the suit to her cheek as if it were a teddy bear.

"Should we go back to the group?" I asked Mike.

"I don't think there's much point."

"I wish we could just cancel this boat thing," I said. But that's the downfall of the guided tour. We couldn't call the shots, because there were other people to consider.

Eventually Manoe rounded us up and told us that our boat was ready. In the massive crowd, a line of people snaked through to board our boat, and I wondered how on earth they managed to keep the right people in the right place, destined for the right boat among dozens that fought for a spot along the dock. I vowed that no matter what happened, I would end up on the same boat as my family.

When we boarded, the realization of the experience sunk in. We were on a three-hour, crowded booze cruise to visit three crowded beaches. I have nothing against booze and nothing against boats, but this wasn't anything we'd have chosen to do, and not only were we doing it, but we were paying someone to facilitate the experience.

The beaches may have been beautiful, but I never got off the boat. Nana took Ivy to shore to walk around at one stop, and at another Mike and Emilia jumped in the water. The waters surrounding the famous beaches of Arraial do Cabo are notoriously cold, confirmed by the look of shock on Mike and Emilia's faces when they jumped in, as well as her repeated shouts of, "Oh my gosh, it's cold, it's cold, it's cold!"

After the cruise, we went back to the van and reluctantly piled back in, tightly packed, everyone's bodies self-consciously squeezed against their neighbors.

"It's about an hour-and-a-half drive to the pousada," Manoe said. *Pousada* was a term we would become intimately familiar with over the next week and a half. It generally implies a small, independently owned B&B or guesthouse. Much like hostels and hotels, the level of comfort and upkeep at a pousada can vary greatly, though on the whole I found them pleasant, adequate, and agreeable. To my delight, they always included clean towels, and I could abandon my practice of blotting myself dry with dirty T-shirts.

As before, Manoe's ETA at the pousada required doubling, so three hours later, the Australian guide, Jennifer, announced, "We're close." The pousada was one that the tour company had never used before, and the driver and guides had considerable difficulty locating it. This was compounded because it was long after dark before we finally reached our destination.

An enthusiastic proprietor greeted us with open arms.

"Hello and welcome!" he shouted. "Welcome to my lovely pousada! I love my pousada, and I love my guests! Welcome, everyone!" If I'd gauged time of day from his energy level, I'd have thought it was noon, not approaching midnight. He seemed genuinely joyful at our presence and set about showing us to our rooms (with plenty of clean towels) and squeezing fresh orange juice so that we could have a midnight round of screwdrivers to forget about the trials of the day. Our room was clean and quaint, a queen bed for Mike and me, perpendicular to a single bed where Emilia would sleep, and another single on wheels rolled out from under our bed for Ivy.

"Ivy's bed is like a ninja bed," Emilia said.

"I hope I don't roll away in the night," said Ivy.

"I'm pretty sure you'll be fine," I assured her.

The next morning, we met in the lobby and readied ourselves to head into town. Búzios was a small fishing village until the 1960s when Brigitte Bardot visited, and ever after it's been one of Brazil's hottest resort towns and a popular destination for those looking to escape the hectic life and pace in Rio.

"The van should be here in just a few minutes," Manoe said.

We stood with our girls, who'd displayed admirable patience from the start of our Brazilian adventure, as if there was something in the air that immediately slowed the body's apprehension and calmed the nerves.

"How about some jumping jacks while we wait?" Mike suggested. He's long been a fan of getting our kids to do jumping jacks and push-ups, often when they complain of boredom and out of curiosity to see if they'll actually do it.

"Okay," said Ivy. "How many?"

"How about twenty," he suggested.

"How about thirty," she countered.

"Okay."

And a small group of us stood and counted for Ivy while she did thirty jumping jacks. I became reacquainted with jumping jacks only once in adulthood, but before that probably hadn't done them since being forced to do so during gym class as a child. After I had children, I hired a trainer to help me get back in shape. He suggested we do a warm-up, and jumping jacks were a part of that routine. I did about three before I stopped.

"What's wrong?" the trainer had asked.

"We need to find something else. Anything else. But I can't do jumping jacks."

"Why not?" he asked.

"Um, I'll be right back," I said and dashed off to the bathroom. It was my first introduction to the unfortunate state of a post-baby body, which threatens to leak urine during every sneeze. Jumping jacks were a surefire way for me to wet my pants.

While Ivy moved on to squats and lunges, Jennifer approached. She moved with a casual nature, but it seemed forced, the sort of posture that implies an agenda. She chatted nonchalantly for a minute, then paused, and I knew she was about to get to whatever it was she *really* wanted to talk about.

"You know, I keep hearing all of these grumblings about people being unhappy," she said, likely referring to the group's general discontent with how the tour had gone so far. Because of the gross miscalculations of travel times and wait times, most of us were doubting our guides' basic abilities to navigate and direct the tours. "I'm not even sure what to do about that Chilean family. I can't make people get along." After chatting for another minute, I realized that she was completely blind to her own shortcomings and instead singled out the Chilean family as responsible for any failures of the tour.

"Gosh," I said. "I hadn't noticed anything about the Chilean family. They seem really nice." This wasn't the confirmation Jennifer had been looking for, and she moved on to attempt gossip somewhere else.

When the van arrived, we took advantage of the transportation to drop us off in downtown Búzios but then set off on our own, grateful for a little distance from the discord of the group.

"I think I might have to get a bikini," my mother-in-law said. "This looks like the place to do it."

"We should all keep our eyes out for a bank, too," my father-in-law added. "We're low on cash."

"The ATM battle continues," I said.

"There's a bank right there," Mike said.

I looked in the direction of his gaze, expecting to see the familiar HSBC, Citibank, or Banco do Brasil signs but saw nothing.

"Where?" I asked. "I don't see it."

"That building right there," Mike said.

"You mean the one with the giant cross on it?"

"Oh. Not a bank?"

"I'm pretty sure that's a church."

We walked on, and my in-laws drifted off into various bikini shops.

"Mom, wait!" Emilia said, letting go of my hand. "I saw an emerald. I have to go back and get it." She returned to me a moment later, holding a shard of green glass.

"Emilia, that's a broken beer bottle," Mike informed her.

"So it's not a treasure?"

"Nope."

"Aw, man."

Downtown Búzios was a shoppers' paradise, with streets and alleyways packed with shops and restaurants. After strolling around town for a few hours, trying to keep the girls from surreptitiously filling their pockets with glass shards, we decided to meet up with the others, sure that the relaxed day and an afternoon of cocktails had cooled tempers and soothed nerves.

We met at a fancy beach club where the girls could play

in the surf, and waiters brought drinks to patrons as they sprawled on giant, futon-like mattresses carved into the hillside overlooking the bay. We chatted, drank, and indulged in octopus carpaccio. Everyone was happy. Except for the octopus.

We'd been told that the evening had been set aside for a traditional Brazilian barbeque, or *churrasco*, hosted by our enthusiastic proprietor at the pousada.

"So, the dinner tonight is free. And if you want some alcohol, you can bring your own," Manoe informed us. The tour had been touted as "super inclusive," and I'd been waiting to find out exactly what that meant. Maybe the dinner would be the start of many perks.

A few hours later, as we gathered around the pousada's courtyard, Manoe approached us. "So, he's telling me that you can't bring your own alcohol, after all," she said. "He has some for sale, though."

"Oh."

"And he has ceviche and soft drinks for sale, too," she added.

"Well, what is included?" I asked.

"Just the meat," she said. Our joyful pousada proprietor was in full business mode.

We milled about and sampled the fare, which included meat, salty meat, extra salty meat, sausage, and meat. Emilia and Ivy played with the Chilean kids, undaunted by their lack of common language.

"I think we're going to head back into town," said Oren, the Canadian against whom I'd been plastered for hours in the van the day before. Oren and Heather were about ten years younger than Mike and me. "Do you guys have any interest in joining us?"

"You guys should go," my mother-in-law encouraged. "We'll watch the girls."

Oren, Heather, Mike, and I returned to Búzios for a glimpse of the nightlife and eventually settled in at an outdoor table along the promenade. The sidewalk ended in an abrupt wall where one could look over the edge into the water of the harbor. Periodic cutouts in the cement allowed the occasional palm to grow, and the setting was pleasant. We ordered a Greek appetizer plate, eager for something other than the meat and sausages we'd been offered at our not-quite-included-with-your-tour-price barbeque.

We watched as a stray dog approached a pile of trash bags, not the giant trash bags we're accustomed to in the States but small shopping bags that had been relegated to trash bags. The dog sniffed through the pile, then apparently made his choice, as if choosing from a platter of canapés. He delicately picked up the bag in his mouth and trotted off down the street.

A moment later, we heard a commotion coming from the restaurant, and I couldn't imagine what could be taking place inside. A fight? Or was I hearing happy sounds? Maybe someone was proposing marriage to his date in the restaurant. Our curiosity was sated as we watched a small opossum run out of the restaurant, cross the sidewalk, and scamper up into one of the spindly palms that dotted the marina.

There was another commotion a minute later as a group of people huddled at the sidewalk's edge, staring into the water. We went to look and saw that people were marveling at a sea turtle swimming lazily about.

"Oh my gosh, that's so awesome!" I said.

"Hmm. It's probably trying to come to shore to die," Mike said.

I elbowed him in the ribs. "Don't you dare ruin this for me."

At two o'clock in the morning, Heather and Oren were ordering shots of tequila. Had we been ten years younger, we might have joined them, but instead we bade them farewell and hailed a cab back to the pousada. We relieved my mother-in-law of her duty of watching over the girls as they slept and turned in.

We rose early the next morning, packed up, and boarded the bus. From there on out, it would be a driver named Marcello, Manoe, and our group of six. We were setting off on our own.

* * *

Lessons in Patience

Patience is bitter but its fruit is sweet.

—Aristotle

The Brazilian landscape was one of geographical beauty, graffiti, and Hortifruti shops. I was sure that Hortifruti shops sold a delicious array of fruits and vegetables, but my affinity for the stores was more because of the word *Hortifruti.* Saying it made me feel both silly and satisfied. Sidewalks held periodic metal platforms raised off the ground on narrow poles. People placed their trash on these platforms, I assumed to deter rats and strays, like the dog we'd seen the night before. Small towns had rows of shops with apartments overtop. We passed bus stops where people waited patiently for transportation. A man waited at one, a typical worker with briefcase in hand, save for the fact that he had no shirt and wore flip-flops. I saw my name on occasion, in a shoe store with "Amanda" in its title, alongside a logo with a pair of six-inch heels, which was a good indication that I wouldn't be shopping there. With the traffic of Arraial do Cabo and petty squabbles far behind us, we stretched out in the bus where we now had two or three seats per person, and Brazil felt lovely again.

As we passed through a small town, Manoe directed Marcello to pull over at an ATM, but when he stopped, I was doubtful. I didn't see the words I needed (HSBC, Citibank, or Banco do Brasil).

"I don't think this is going to work," I told Manoe. "It has to be one of those three for our international cards to work."

"It should work," she assured me. "This is a national bank."

Certain we weren't communicating, I resolved to try just in case. My mother-in-law and I exited the van and approached the bank, from which stretched an enormous line.

"You don't have to wait in the line," Manoe said. "That's for people waiting for the branch to open up. You just need the ATM line. It's much shorter."

That was reassuring, but I was still convinced our cards wouldn't work at these machines. The ATM line ran parallel to the other line, and at one point I waited alongside a woman who stood with her eyes closed and appeared to be sleeping while standing up and waiting for the bank to open. She looked like she was used to the situation and had perfected this means of passing the time. As my mother-in-law and I neared the front of the line, we saw countless people before us attempt transactions with the machines, then eventually shake their heads in frustration and walk away. I assumed this meant they were malfunctioning or out of funds. When it was my turn, I approached, went through the process, and received the error message I'd expected. On a whim, I decided to try one more time, this time requesting half as much money, and I was shocked when the machine produced cash for me. I repeated the process with another card, then told my mother-in-law the trick. I'd been sure that the machines would not work for us, and in the end, it appeared they worked *only* for us.

Back in the van, I was mesmerized by the passing landscape of chickens and railroad tracks and narrow roads flanked by giant bamboo. Lush, green mountains jutted from the earth in odd forms and angles, and the ground seemed to rest in droops and bends as if in a Salvador Dali painting.

We stopped briefly at a gas station and convenience store, giving us the opportunity to use the bathroom and grab a snack if we chose. At a counter, we viewed the typical pastels and other meat-filled, fried offerings. The meat consumption of Brazil was slightly beyond my comfort zone, but this menu offered pastels filled with spinach, and another with hearts of palm. None of those appeared to be in the actual case of food, though, so I decided to ask, and in Portuguese said, *"Você tem pastel sem carne?"* (Do you have pastel without meat?). The response in Portuguese was *"Sim. Frango e camarão."* To her, these were the meat-free offerings, the ones with chicken and shrimp, and the menu items advertising spinach and hearts of palm were just to tease any passing vegetarians.

Convenience stores were great places to view Brazil's antismoking campaign. Cigarettes were for sale, but to purchase them you would first be confronted by a variety of posters dissuading you from doing so. (Though there isn't really anything you can put on a poster that will dissuade a true smoker from smoking.) Brazil put forth a valiant effort, though. One poster showed a half-naked man standing, his head hanging in shame. In the foreground, his naked lower half was covered by a woman's hand in the thumbs-down position, indicating that if you smoke, you will be a terrible disappointment to a woman in the bedroom, and despite any efforts to the contrary, you will find your penis sadly pointing limply to the floor (in the direction of the woman's thumb). Another campaign depicted a father (the smoker) dying in a hospital bed while his devastated son stood helplessly next to him. Again, the intent is to show you how much you will disappoint those who love you if you continue to smoke and then selfishly die on them because you couldn't quit cigarettes.

We continued along the BR101, past abandoned buildings and shacks along railroad tracks. We saw farmland and cattle with giant humps on their backs, drove by mammoth rock faces, cliffs of exposed red earth, and sugarcane fields. After hours on the road, we pulled into a rest stop for lunch. It was the common Brazilian buffet, with meat, beans, rice, beets, sweet plantains, and various salads. I was joyful at the sight of vegetables and loaded my plate. While the Brazilian buffets are often good, their system's lack of efficiency is an indication of Brazil's overall inefficiency. When you enter the dining hall, an employee hands you a small card or device. After you fill your plate, it is then weighed, and someone takes your card to either electronically or manually assign the pricing for your food to the card. After you eat, you take the card to another stop, where someone converts your card into a bill to be paid. Then you must take this bill to the cashier, which is the final checkpoint for you to complete the transaction before you are permitted to leave.

At a roundabout as we drove through the town of Campos, the road circled a small patch of grass, on which I spied a stray dog. It appeared as if curled up and sleeping. But as our van turned around to the other side, I saw that the dog had no eyes, and a vulture approached then to feast on the dead creature.

My gaze moved from the dog to a woman who rode by on a bike, navigating it while also holding a sleeping toddler.

"We're going to stop at a store so you can get anything you might need," Manoe said. "The next pousada is very remote, so you can't just walk to town for a store."

Mike and I looked at his parents, and we all went through the mental checklist of alcohol and mixers to stock up on. My father-in-law agreed to stay in the van with the girls and the driver while Mike, his mother, Manoe, and I went inside. In addition to alcohol, I replenished our bottled water, searched out snacks for the girls, and ran with open arms to the produce section.

"Look," I said to Mike. "We can get *apples*."

At the checkout, we placed our items on the counter, until I put the bag of apples there, and the checker looked at me, shook her head, and pointed for me to leave. It seemed a cruel act, to give me a glimpse of hope for fresh produce containing some nutritional value, and then tell me that no, I would only be allowed to eat meat, french fries, and fried squares of dough during my two months in Brazil.

The checker explained herself, but in Portuguese that went far beyond my basic proficiency, and Manoe was still shopping in other parts of the store.

"Okay," I said to Mike and his mother. "You guys keep going. Apparently I have to pay for these somewhere else. I'll try and figure it out."

"Well, okay," Mike said reluctantly. At first I thought he feared for me, as if I might get lost or abducted in my quest to purchase apples, but he was worried for himself. I was his walking phrasebook, and Manoe was still out of sight. He knew that between him and his mother, their communication would be reduced to sign language and butchered Spanish, in the hopes that it was similar enough to communicate a basic message.

"Just nod, smile, and hand over your credit card," I instructed, and took my apples away.

I approached a new checker, a young man, and he looked at me with my bag of apples and shook his head. I asked him in Portuguese, "Where?" and pointed to the other check-ers. "I want to pay," I said. My accent and complete lack of understanding clued him into the fact that I was likely foreign and didn't know how things worked, as opposed to just an obstinate customer who refused to follow protocol. He said something to another checker one lane over, then stood and motioned for me to follow him. He led me back to the produce section, and for a moment I feared he was going to make me return the apples to the bin from which I took them. Maybe the apples weren't for sale, or I had to purchase a special permit for them, or something about me wasn't good enough to allow me such an indulgence. But then I saw, in the middle of the produce section, an employee standing behind a counter. On the counter, between the employee and shoppers, was a scale. And it all made sense. The checker took my apples, handed them to the Lord of Weighing Fruits, and said something about my lack of understanding, to which they shared a good chuckle.

"You figure it out?" Mike asked upon my return.

"Barely."

"Way to persevere."

"I'm determined to get us healthy again," I said. "Between the apples and where we're headed, I figure we're on track."

"What's special about where we're headed?"

"Didn't you read the itinerary Manoe sent us?"

"What itinerary? There's an itinerary?"

"Never mind," I said, realizing the itinerary languished in my inbox where I'd failed to forward it to anyone in our party. "In any case, there's something in the environment of the next town we're going to that's supposed to be really good for you."

"Like what?" he prompted.

A fair question, given my vague and unsatisfying description. What could make an environment good for you? Pristine air? Vitamins and minerals in the water? Or did they have city-wide bans on unhealthy vices? I panicked at the thought of there being prohibitions on alcohol. Should we all start carrying hip flasks just in case? But surely such a thing as a "dry town" could never exist in Brazil.

"I'm not sure," I answered. "I guess we'll find out when we get there."

* * *

Guarapari

Brazilian beaches may be famous for solar radiation (among other things) but strollers on Guarapari's pristine white sand shores may want to apply sunscreen to their soles as well.

—"Hot Spots: Earth's 5 Most Naturally Radioactive Places,"
Web Ecoist

"Do you see the two mountains who look at each other?" Manoe asked, pointing to the horizon. "That's where we're going."

We'd driven by hills of tiered earth, leaving the state of Rio de Janeiro and entering Espirito Santo. I marveled at the mountains along the drive, the occasional spears of earth jutting from the land, and was intrigued by the fact that our next accommodations would be located a fair drive up one of the giant hillsides.

"Manoe?" my father-in-law asked. Although for some reason he suddenly changed the pronunciation of her name. He didn't say ma-NOO, as she'd taught us and how he'd pronounced her name for the previous few days. He now switched to ma-NOW. This was also interesting in that the entire time we'd traveled in and out of Manaus, pronounced ma-NOWS, he'd called it MANus. "How much longer until we get there?"

"Probably about thirty minutes," she said, ignoring his sudden change of her name. We translated this to mean an hour.

The municipality of Iconha in Espirito Santo is famous for bananas, though we also passed endless crops of coffee beans, sugarcane, strawberries, and grapes. As the crops grew thicker on either side of the road, Marcello began speaking to Manoe, who translated for us.

"He says that it may look like these are all different wild crops growing," said Manoe. "You'll see lots of banana trees that look like they're growing in the jungle, but every tree is actually owned by someone. So you don't necessarily just want to help yourself to what you find." I had images of being threatened with a shotgun for reaching for a banana and was thankful I'd purchased the apples, no matter the hassle of paying for them.

We reached the hillside pousada where Mike, Emilia, Ivy, and I were shown into a hostel-type room. It was large with lockers against one wall so that backpackers might lock up their belongings if sharing a room with strangers. Mike and I would sleep on two twin beds pushed together to form a makeshift queen while Ivy and Emilia had bunk beds against the wall opposite the lockers. The room had more space than we'd need and included a small kitchenette and fridge. My in-laws had a smaller room on the other side of the building, with a tiny balcony facing another huge cliff, overlooking an expansive gorge that ran far below.

After checking in, we gathered in the main meeting space and dining hall of the bed-and-breakfast.

"Mom, I really want to hike that mountain," Emilia said, pointing to the mass of earth on the other side of the gorge.

"We can do that, if you like," said Manoe. "It's a really great day hike."

Mike and I instinctively looked at one another, silently agreeing that there was no way in hell we'd make it up that mountain, let alone with our kids in tow.

The owners of the pousada, a French couple, were there, and my mother-in-law complimented them on the place.

The woman remained silent, not fluent in English, while the man spoke proficiently with a lilting French accent.

"Well, you can buy it. It's for sale." There was a weary aspect to his voice, as if he wanted nothing more than to be rid of the picturesque hillside pousada. I thought that it must often be that way, with people carrying a romanticized vision of what it's like to own and run a bed-and-breakfast and then finding themselves burned out in just a few short years, exhausted by the duties of hosting.

"Listen," he turned to Manoe, "I have so much to do right now. And I have to get everything ready for the dinner this evening. I'm so tired, and for me to prepare everything for you guys, well it's really just a lot of work."

Suddenly we wished to be anywhere but there. This would be the first of many instances in which he made clear that our presence was a burden, whether it was his job or not. Despite his countenance, at the dinner that night, where far more than just meat was included in the price of our stay, he made the best churrasco we'd had in Brazil, cooking on a tiny outdoor grill on the narrow patio off the dining hall. He prepared the requisite steak and sausages, supplemented with tilapia, an African salad, and barbequed bananas and pineapples for dessert. When serving his guests and receiving well-deserved praise for his culinary skills, he beamed. The weariness of before dissipated, and I thought I caught a glimpse of the part of him that had been drawn to being a proprietor in the first place. His wife worked diligently in the kitchen, occasionally stealing glances at us and other patrons with narrowed, suspicious eyes. I attributed this to her own feelings of burnout but also the exclusion of not understanding any of the ongoing communication while her husband chatted merrily away.

The town of Guarapari was a twenty-minute cab ride away. Along with the incredible views and mountain backdrop, we would remember our time there equally for the food. In addition to our hosts' fantastic barbeque, our days included meals at restaurants in town. At one, my in-laws ordered the steak parmigiana, a popular offering wherever we went. Steak was breaded, fried, and covered in marinara sauce and cheese. My husband ordered a steak covered in fried eggs. It goes without saying that I married into a family that loves protein. The year before, at a family get-together with Mike's sister and her family, our eldest niece was recovering from the flu, and her mother, my sister-in-law, was encouraging her daughter to eat.

"You need more steak, Bella," she said. "You're sick, and your body needs protein."

I'm well aware of the fact that different cultures and even families within those cultures hold different beliefs on the proper remedies for ailments. But I'd thought that in our typical American culture, we all agreed on lots of fluids and vitamin C. I'd never before heard (nor have I since) that a flu-afflicted youth is best served with a hearty filet.

Manoe solved the riddle of the town's health benefits by imparting to us the intriguing yet disturbing information that

Guarapari has naturally high levels of radiation and that lots of people flock to the beaches in the hopes of curing cancer. I wasn't sure at the time if I was hearing rumor, an old wives' tale, or something that had been terribly mixed up in translation. I would later learn that it was true. Along with Guarapari in Brazil, Iran, India, Australia, and China each have a city known for natural high background radiation. Visiting these areas is thought (by some) to come with health benefits, like longer life span. Conversely, living in these areas is thought (by some) to increase a resident's risk of dying of cancer.

"Guarapari also has the most churches and bars per inhabitant," our proprietor said before shuffling us into a cab. I wasn't sure if any of the information they were giving us was meant to be reassuring or distressing.

Mike sat in the front seat while my in-laws and I sat in the back, with the girls on our laps.

"Mom," Ivy said as the cabbie navigated the winding road from the hillside down into central Guarapari, "do you know how someone could die at a birthday party?"

"Uh . . ."

"If they had a knife to cut the cake and then instead they cut up their whole body."

"Uh . . ." I didn't know how else to respond and instead left it at that, grateful that our cab driver spoke no English.

Guarapari is home to many beaches, and we located a spot on a narrow one where children frolicked in the water and climbed great jumbles of rocks jutting up from the sand. As in Rio, we had little trouble locating inexpensive chairs and umbrellas for rent, as well as vendors selling caipirinhas, corn on the cob, fried cheese on a stick, and other snacks and souvenirs.

"Oh, look, Mom! Tattoos!" Emilia said.

"Can we get one?" asked Ivy.

"We'll see," I said, which they correctly processed as both vague and unsatisfying. After a moment, I reconsidered. Not only had the prices in Brazil been exceedingly cheap when compared to those in America, but most of our purchases thus far had been geared toward making the adults comfortable and providing for their indulgences. I had no desire to curb my indulgences and instead decided the best thing to do to assuage my guilt would be to get something for the girls to level the playing field.

"I'm going to walk the girls over to the tattoos," I said to Mike. "And maybe let them pick one out."

It goes without saying, of course, that these were of the temporary variety. The only problem with the temporary tattoo stand was that there were too many tattoos. Thousands of designs were displayed on five large boards perched up and leaning against one another to form a mini-pentagon of tattoos. From Disney characters to flaming swords to scantily clad women to Chinese symbols, all of the clichéd tattoos were there, along with some more imaginative ones. My daughters have been known to take twenty minutes to decide which apple slice to eat first. This myriad of choices overwhelmed them. After fifteen minutes of circling the tattoos and looking at each one, they made their decisions.

"I think I want this one," Emilia said, indicating a large, snarling tiger.

"And I think I want this one," Ivy said, pointing to a princess. At first glance, I saw a normal princess, but on closer inspection I saw the princess's plunging neckline and exposed thigh and decided that she was more temptress than princess.

"Which ones did you pick out?" Mike asked, having wandered over from our beach spot, wondering what was taking us so long.

"Emilia wants the giant, angry tiger, and Ivy wants a really inappropriate princess," I said, motioning to the tattoos they wanted.

"What are you two—sailors?" Mike asked. "How about something different."

After another fifteen minutes of deliberation, we talked them into alternate tattoos involving hearts and flowers and butterflies, images that would be slightly less likely to indicate their allegiance to a biker gang or prison brotherhood.

"Look, Nana and Papa," Ivy said when all was said and done and we returned to the group.

"So pretty," my mother-in-law cooed obligatorily. Then she turned to me. "Want to go get a drink?" Which is one reason why I love her. We left Mike and his father in charge of the girls and wandered over to a makeshift beach bar where we ordered two caipirinhas. By this point in the trip, we'd learned to order them with a great emphasis on very little sugar to counter the Brazilian instinct to dump half a cup of sugar in each cocktail. The bartender was a cheerful man in his sixties who expertly made the drinks and handed them to my mother-in-law to hold while I fished through my wallet to pay. After I'd done so, I turned to my mother-in-law and, before taking the drink from her hand, plucked from it a long hair. The bartender saw this, immediately grabbed a bottle of vodka, and topped the drink off with a shot of booze, as if to compensate for the offensive hair. I accepted this compensation.

Both Manoe and the owner of the pousada had given us the name of a restaurant they would be at that evening, at which we were welcome to join them. We had a map of Guarapari with a vague notion of where the restaurant was located. We wandered through town, occasionally asking strangers if they knew where we might find the restaurant called Valdecy. Most of them were tourists themselves, or there for the literally radiant beaches in the hopes of staving off cancer, and couldn't help us. Eventually a man on a bicycle nodded with comprehension and motioned for us to follow him. He rode slowly so that our group might keep up. Would he lead us into a dark alley where thugs waited to mug us? Or worse? Or would he take us to our destination and then demand a tip of extortionate magnitude? We continued following him, and my panic increased as the landscape around us grew more industrial and deserted.

"I'm not sure this is the side of town we want to be in," I said.

"Well, let's just go with it," said Mike.

"There it is," said my father-in-law.

The man nodded, pointed at the restaurant, and simply wished us well. It was a tiny restaurant with more tables outside than in, a rough-around-the-edges watering hole and eatery that catered to locals but welcomed us as the rare exception. The menu was a giant metal sign affixed to the front of the building that listed Valdecy's offerings.

Manoe and the proprietor sat with a few others at an outdoor table, and the six of us took another table nearby. When the pousada owner asked if we trusted him to order for us, we nodded without hesitation. A short time later, we were presented with enormous plates of fish and pork and beef, all accompanied by huge platters of rice and beans and french fries, more food than would fit comfortably on the table and certainly more than we could eat.

"I think that's the guy who showed us how to get here," Mike said, motioning to a man sitting by himself a few tables away. "I'm going to buy him a beer."

Mike is not known for willingly interacting with people outside of his immediate comfort zone, especially if the person in question doesn't speak English, but a caipirinha or two had changed that and inspired in him feelings of gratitude. He approached the man, pointed at the beer and said the name of it, then motioned for a waiter to bring the man another and add it to our bill. The man showed Mike gratitude in return, in the only way he could, with smiles and a nod of the head in thanks.

When Mike returned to the table, the pousada owner attempted to explain some of the dishes to us. He did so in 90 percent English and 10 percent Portuguese.

"They make this," he indicated the beef dish, "from this part of the boy." He motioned to his calf.

And I silently lamented the fact that while eating, I now had the image in my head of consuming meat made from the legs of little boys.

"And they make this," he pointed at another dish, "from the *juice* of this part of the boy." *Boi* in Portuguese can mean beef, and by "juice" of the leg, he meant bone marrow. We nodded, smiled, thanked him for all of his help, and I focused on the fish.

* * *

Attack of the Birthday Beetles

We hope that, when the insects take over the world, they will remember with gratitude how we took them along on all our picnics.

—Bill Vaughan

The next morning, I woke early and left Mike sleeping while creeping over to the girls' bunk beds. "Girls," I whispered. Their eyes fluttered open, and they looked at me with the familiar confusion regarding our surroundings. They looked around the room, reminding themselves of our current accommodations, then refocused on me. "Today's Dad's birthday," I said. "Should we give him our presents?"

Before leaving America, we knew that both Nana and Mike would have birthdays during our Brazilian adventures. They had a card, homemade bracelet, and Darth Vader (or Dark Vader, according to my daughters) keychain ready to give to their father.

"Let's get the stuff," I whispered. They hopped down from the bunk beds and hastily donned beach dresses. I handed Ivy the card and keychain, wrapped haphazardly in tissue paper, and Emilia the bracelet she'd made. They began a slow march toward their father, singing "Happy Birthday." Mike opened his eyes to see his daughters singing to him and holding out their gifts.

Hours later, when we again found ourselves soaking in the sun and radiation of Guarapari's beaches, my in-laws disappeared for half an hour into town before returning and presenting Mike with a bag. Inside was a fancy button-down shirt, almost iridescent in color with a purplish hue.

"Happy birthday, son," his mom said.

"It was *really* expensive," added his dad. "I mean, everything in Brazil has been so cheap, and we somehow managed to find the most expensive store and pick out the most expensive thing in there."

"No!" I interrupted, more sharply than I'd intended. "You don't get to do that. You don't get to give someone a gift along with the guilt trip of how much it cost you."

"Oh," said my father-in-law. "I mean, happy birthday, son."

When we later said goodbye to the owner of the pousada, who now seemed genuinely kind and friendly while also somewhat relieved that he'd have fewer guests to deal with, Manoe and the host agreed that we would take with our group a Brazilian couple and drop them off at a nearby town, which was on our intended route. We had plenty of room in the van and readily agreed. The couple spoke no English, and we communicated with them in the little Portuguese that I did know, supplemented with friendly expressions and body language.

We passed the historical town of Vila Velha and drove by huge expanses of beach and high-end promenades. Highrises and condos were everywhere as we neared Vitoria, and it was evident that we were in an area of rapid growth and development.

"Over there is Frog Rock," Manoe said. And we looked out to the sea where a rock, in the unmistakable shape of a frog, appeared to hover above the waves.

The Brazilian woman was obviously familiar with Frog Rock and asked Manoe how to say "frog" in English.

"Frog," Manoe said slowly.

"Flog?" the woman asked.

"Frog," Manoe repeated.

"Flog?"

"Frog."

The Brazilian woman nodded then, as if this time she had it, then said. "Ah, *sim*, flog." We dropped them off in Vitoria and bade them farewell.

It was six more hours to Itaúnas, the last leg of which included a twenty-seven-kilometer drive along a dirt road. When we finally reached the secluded surfer town, we checked into a quaint, small pousada. Towering mango trees surrounded a small pool in the courtyard. The atmosphere was delightful, until a falling mango hit the ground next to me with a horrifying thud. I spent the rest of our time there in fear that I would die from falling fruit.

That night, still Mike's birthday, I was excited about the activities before us. First we would have a caipirinha-making class, and I was eager to learn the nuances of preparing the national drink, which we'd more than embraced during our trip. This would be followed by a *forro* class, instruction on a typical Brazilian dance. I was less excited about this, as I'm a far better drinker than I am a dancer.

Manoe was our instructor for the caipirinha class, and on the outdoor table of the pousada, covered by a roof and therefore safe from the kamikaze mangoes, she set up a few bowls of chips on which to snack as well as all of the items we'd need to make our caipirinhas. These included cups, ice, vodka, a cocktail shaker, screwdriver, limes, sugar, cachaça, and passion fruit. A traditional caipirinha is just lime, but she'd asked if we liked any of the variations, and I'd readily volunteered my love for passion fruit.

"Who's going first?" she asked.

"Me!" Emilia cried. "Please pick me!"

As discussed ahead of time, the girls would participate and make themselves virgin versions of the national drink, basically limeade.

"I think the birthday boy should go first," I said.

"Oh, you're right," Emilia conceded. "Dad, it's your birthday so you get to go first."

Mike approached the table, and Manoe walked him through the process. "First, you're going to cut a lime into sections and cut out the middle white part. You put that in the shaker and now add your sugar. Brazilians like them *so* sweet, but you can add as much as you want." Mike added the equivalent of a quarter of a teaspoon of sugar to the shaker. "Now you'll take this," she held up the screwdriver, "and you're going to mulch it." She meant muddle, and in the absence of an actual muddle, we had a screwdriver. Mike held the screwdriver upside down and shoved the tool's handle into the bottom of the cocktail shaker to squeeze the juice from the lime. "Next, you're going to add a scoop of ice." He did so. "And now the alcohol. A traditional caipirinha is made with cachaça, which is an alcohol made from sugarcane." She indicated the bottle of cachaça. "But you can make a version with vodka if you'd prefer that. It's very common here also, sometimes called a caipiroska or a caipivodka, so it's up to you."

"I'll go with the casasha," Mike said.

"Cachaça," Manoe corrected. "Okay, so the way they measure it here is to count when it has this type of top on the bottle. And you're going to count to seven." Mike did so at a respectable pace, not too fast, nor was he going to shortchange himself on the alcoholic content of his beverage. "And then you shake it. And the way to tell if you've shaken it enough is that you shake it until the shaker is so cold that you can't hold on to it anymore." Mike dutifully shook, effectively melting some of the ice, the importance of which I realized, now that I saw that the only liquid in a caipirinha, other than the alcohol, was a little bit of lime juice and whatever bit of water melted from the ice. "Now pour it into your cup and there you go."

The process was not a quick one, and by the time the next person had mixed their drink, Mike's was already empty, but we went down the line with patience, Emilia and Ivy making for themselves a mix of lime, sugar, water, and ice, and pleased with themselves for the grown-up opportunities of cutting a lime and mixing a drink.

When it was my mother-in-law's turn, and it came time for her to count to seven while pouring the alcohol, she seemed to go into a trance once she reached the number four, adding booze for an additional five seconds before reluctantly counting out, "five . . . six . . . and six and a half . . . seven."

The caipirinhas were delicious, and we were free to continue making and drinking them when the dance instructor showed up. He was a tall, friendly man in his late forties and with perfect English. *Forro* refers to both a style of music and dance popular in Northeast Brazil. The teacher gave us a few simple steps and played music from a cassette tape and player he'd brought with him. Ivy attempted for approximately fifteen seconds before deciding instead to pout and sit in the corner with her arms crossed. Maybe she'd had one too many cups of limeade. Mike and I followed along with little trouble, as the steps were very simple, while my in-laws, known for being fantastic dancers, seemed to struggle and wanted the moves shown to them multiple times. This confused me, given their natural talent. Eventually I concluded that the dance was too simple for them and that it might have gone better if the instructor had led them in a more advanced version. After a time, they gave up on following the forro steps and resorted to their usual swing style.

After a few lessons, we took a break to replenish our drinks. I approached the table to find four beetles slowly trudging amid the limes and bottles of booze. I flicked them off of the table just as Mike said, "Look at all these beetles." He motioned to the floor and the chairs scattered about.

"Mom, there's a bug on me!" Ivy shrieked. And the presence of the beetle on her arm erased all of her intentions of sulking silently in the corner. I flicked it away from her, just as a beetle flew into my face, bouncing off the middle of my forehead. Beetles were everywhere, on every surface and person, and I wondered if this was a nightly occurrence or unexpected phenomenon. Beetles are better than any other number of insects, though. They are slow and plodding, unlike roaches that dart with startling speed. And most beetles don't bite, unlike mosquitoes. As unpleasant as the sudden swarm of creatures was, I recognized that it could have been much worse. As quickly as they appeared, the influx stopped, and after two minutes with a broom, the patio was clear. I wouldn't think about the beetles again until three hours later, while taking a shower, when I found a beetle nestled in my hair. It was not the best shower I've had.

The next morning, we ate breakfast at the pousada before gathering to meet Manoe, who led us on a short walk into town. At a tour office, we met with a guide who would lead us on a three-hour kayak trip in the Itaúnas River. The idea of a three-hour kayak trip with two children under the age of ten was daunting. What if someone got queasy or fell in? What if the whining reached such proportions that our guide couldn't take it and purposely abandoned us on a remote tributary? What if the water was rough and scary? But the water was shallow and still, resembling a long, narrow pond more than a flowing river. Our guide made us all wear life jackets, about which my father-in-law was less than thrilled but for which I was grateful.

Mike and I each had a child seated in front of us in our kayaks, and we gave the girls turns paddling. At one point, we stopped at a small island, where the guide pointed out cashew trees and capybara trails. The capybara is the largest rodent in the world, sort of like a mutant guinea pig and therefore something I desperately wanted to see, though the creatures eluded us. Our guide climbed a palm and retrieved a young coconut. He skittered down the tree, smacked the coconut on a rock until it split, and we held out our empty water bottles as he gave us each a few ounces of coconut water. By the end of the kayak trip, both girls were sleeping in our laps as we paddled back. They seemed rested enough when we returned to shore that we decided to venture to the beach instead of returning to the pousada.

"Oh, yes," Manoe said. "You should definitely go check out the beach and the dunes that Itaúnas is famous for. It's only about a ten-minute walk, and it's beautiful. The old town is buried under the dunes, and you can still see the church steeple sticking up." There is something magical and claustrophobic about a city under the sand, and while I recognized the beauty and power of nature, I also choked a little and thought of Pompeii.

We made our way along the road toward the dunes. The road gave way to a trail that eventually narrowed through a forested area, then opened up to the base of a steep dune. Along the forested track, we passed trees afflicted with giant termite nests.

"Watch this," my father-in-law said as we passed one. He took a stick and punctured the nest. Thousands of termites scurried out.

My mother-in-law shuddered and said, "I don't think I needed to see that particular image. It gives me the jeepers creepers."

"You mean the heebie jeebies?" I asked. "Or the willies?"

"Yes," she confirmed, "all of that."

The area was both popular and treacherous enough that someone had installed a giant rope down the incline of the dune so that trekkers could pull themselves up. A quarter of the way to the top, my thighs and lungs burned. We were drenched in sweat and practically dragging the children. I reminded myself that our guide, Manoe, was extremely fit. She was young, exercised regularly, and refrained from the indulgences of fried food and alcohol to which our group was prone. The next time she mentioned that something was just a ten-minute walk, we would take her recommendation with suspicion.

When we finally crested the dune, we were confronted with more dunes, and our group shared a collective groan.

"It's like something out of *Star Wars*," Mike said. "No trees, no plants, just dunes and sand and heat."

"Whatever you do, don't take your shoes off," warned Emilia. "The sand is so hot."

I kicked off one of my flip-flops, sure that she was overreacting, and instantly felt the bottoms of my feet burn. "Holy crap, she's right. This *is* like something out of *Star Wars*." I quickly returned my foot to its flip-flop. Ivy then took off her shoes, felt the sand, shrugged, and trotted off to crest the next dune.

When we'd all done so, I was relieved to see the water, having been momentarily convinced that we were doomed to wander among the dunes until we either succumbed to dehydration or were captured by the clone army. Upon reaching the water's edge, we kicked off our flip-flops and cooled our feet in the surf.

"Mom, do we have to do that same walk back?" Emilia asked.

"I don't know, sweetie," I said truthfully.

"I think we should head that way," said Mike, pointing to his left. Farther down the beach, we saw a bustle of activity, at least in comparison to the relatively deserted swath of beach on which we stood. People were enjoying the water, and a few restaurants speckled the shore.

"You want to go even farther? It's going to be a struggle to make it back as it is." I couldn't imagine the return trip, trudging through the dunes again.

"I think if we go down there, we can relax at one of the restaurants," Mike explained. "Maybe get something to drink and then take the road back from there and bypass the dunes. I think it's a better way to go back."

We all agreed that if there was a way to avoid another trip over the dunes, it was worth it, even if the distance was longer. After another five-minute walk along the water's edge, we arrived at one of the restaurants and sat at a partially shaded table built on a small wooden deck on a dune overlooking the sea. A waiter passed out menus.

"Wait," I said. "Do we have money?"

Manoe had told us we wouldn't need any money for the kayak trip, as it was included in the tour, and had warned us against bringing purses or valuables along, because they might get wet or damaged. We hadn't planned for any money we might need after the kayak trip. We all emptied our pockets and found that with just a few random bills and change, we'd pooled together enough for fries, soda, and a few cans of beer.

The walk back was long and hard and hot but still easier than a return trip trekking over the dunes. We were all due for a shower when we made it back to the pousada, sweaty, melting, and exhausted, but there was no hot water at the time, so the girls and I instead cooled off in the pool.

"I'm still going to take a shower," said Mike.

"You're going to shower with no hot water? Are you even human?" I asked.

"It's kind of invigorating. You should try it."

"I think we both know that's not going to happen."

"Mom *hates* water, Dad," said Ivy. "She's like a cat. Remember?"

"I can't even believe she's in the pool with us," Emilia said quietly.

"Let's not talk about it too much," Ivy stage-whispered to Emilia. "We don't want to scare her away."

That night, the in-laws encouraged us to go into town and offered to watch the girls so that we could do so. Accompanied by Marcello and Manoe, we didn't venture out for long but just enough to lazily wander through a few shops and stop for ice cream.

"Do you want some?" Mike asked.

"No, I just want a bite of whatever you get."

"Okay." He joined Manoe at the counter so that she might translate for him while I looked out over a common area. It was just short of a park but with a few benches where couples sat enjoying the evening respite from the sun.

"You want a bite?" Mike asked a minute later.

"What kind did you get?"

"Guess."

"Coffee?" I ventured hopefully.

"Nope."

"Chocolate?"

"It's something yellow." He flashed me a peek of a yellow scoop of ice cream in his cup.

"It's banana," I said with disappointment. My husband loves banana-flavored things, whereas I just like bananas.

"Nope, not banana."

"Just tell me," I pleaded.

"Here, just take a bite," he said, and as I opened my mouth to protest, he occupied it with a spoonful of ice cream.

"Corn?" I said in disbelief. "Was that corn ice cream you just made me eat?"

"Yeah, do you like it?" He happily ate away.

"I like corn. And I like ice cream. But that's just wrong."

"Oh, come on. Be adventurous."

"I *am* adventurous. In the past two days, I kayaked for

three hours and hiked a dune and learned forro and had beetles nesting in my hair."

"So . . . you want another bite?" he asked.

"I love you so much," I answered, "that I want you to have it."

* * *

If You Like Piña Coladas

Brazil takes the hotdog to another level. Cachorro quente *is served with a variety of toppings to choose from, including mashed potatoes, fried shoestring potatoes, corn, tomatoes, or vinaigrette (chopped tomatoes and onions in olive oil and vinegar).*

—Jenna Francisco, "5 Best Street Foods in Brazil"

As we entered Bahia, the landscape changed with every mile, by turns flat and hilly. We passed farmland as well as shacks along the road that seemed uninhabitable but served as homes. As the rain came down and the van lumbered along, we grew silent, weary of another seven-hour ride. We passed a wrecked van with huge tarps and trash bags covering its damage, like half-assed bandages on an open wound. We stopped for lunch, the ubiquitous Brazilian buffet, where the waitresses couldn't help but touch my daughters' hair.

"*Lindas*!" they always said. The first few times this happened, I wondered if Brazilian women assumed all blonde girls were named Linda. Eventually I figured out that this meant beautiful, and the girls were accustomed to having strangers pet their heads and call them Linda.

Back in the van, we passed a store called the House of Agriculture. It was a large store occupying a wooden,

A-framed structure. There was no furniture inside, just a cement floor with one giant pile of watermelons and one of coconuts. We passed more towering mango trees, shacks with satellite dishes, and stairs carved into steep hillsides of deep red earth.

We arrived weary in Arraial d'Ajuda but perked up when we saw our accommodations, which were nicer with each stop along the tour. We each had our own bed, our own towel, *and* we had hot water. When we'd shaken off the long van ride and everyone felt ready to venture out, Manoe walked us into town.

"First, we'll go to the church," she said.

Mike darted a quick look in my direction, no doubt expecting me to groan or roll my eyes, as I'm apt to do whenever there is any mention of worship, but I kept my reaction in check. I find churches in other countries fascinating studies of culture and architecture, and as long as no one is asking me to confess my sins, I'm happy to take the tour. It turned out that we weren't headed inside the church but rather behind the church. Along the way, Manoe stopped to purchase some brightly colored ribbons of cloth. They were thin and printed with various phrases on them. When we reached the church and walked to the back, where a railing perched along a slight cliff overlooking the water, we saw thousands of these ribbons tied to the railing. It was a riot of colors waving in the breeze coming off the water. It was beautiful.

"So you take one." Manoe offered the ribbons and let us each choose our color. "And you tie three knots, and you make three wishes or prayers. And the saying is that when the ribbon eventually falls off, the wishes come true."

"I want pink!" Ivy hopped up and down.

"I'm going to have to really think about this," Emilia said. "There are so many things to wish for. Like being able to fly or having my own phone. This is going to be a tough one."

"And you can tie them here to the railing, or you can also tie them anywhere, on a backpack, your keychain, wherever you like. You'll see them all around in Bahia."

When we wished, some of us focused on health, happiness, and peace for our loved ones, while others wished for the sudden acquisition of supernatural powers, a flying baby unicorn, and a house made of chocolate. After tying our ribbons, it was time to move on from mythical treats and find some real food.

Arraial d'Ajuda is known for good street food. Carts line up in an open section of town, each with a few plastic tables and chairs set up nearby. The girls opted for hot dogs, and the vendor looked disappointed when I eschewed his various toppings and asked for two hot dogs with only ketchup. Mike chose skewered meat while I tried the *acarajé*, a dish made from black-eyed pea fritters and shrimp, and one that Bahia is known for. We searched out a table and chairs and sat with our food. After a moment, a man approached. Manoe had wandered off, and our table turned to me for a translation.

"I think he's asking us if we're going to buy anything," I said. And then we realized that the tables were not a free for all, but each food cart had a certain number of tables, and if you were going to sit at one, you were expected to purchase something from that particular cart. "If we're going to sit here, we need to buy something from his food stall." These situations were always manageable, because food was cheap and street food was really cheap. We had no problem purchasing a few additional skewers of meat and soft drinks from him.

The food area skirted a common area where performers showcased their talents and then passed around a hat. We watched the performers but then became engrossed in a different show. On the wall of a storefront near our table, a showdown was taking place between a gecko and a cricket. The two perched on the wall just a few inches from each other. I can't say I have much knowledge of the ocular capabilities of either, but it appeared they were in a staring contest.

"Do you think that gecko wants to eat that cricket?" Emilia asked.

"The cricket looks too big," I said. "They're almost the same size."

The gecko darted forth and neatly bit off the cricket's head. The body of the cricket remained on the wall for a moment before falling to the ground, where it continued to move for quite some time. Even after being dislocated, the cricket head looked too big for the gecko to consume, and we watched in a mixture of awe and disgust as the gecko spent the next few minutes swallowing the head, which we could then see moving inside the gecko's body. I worried that my children might be scarred from the sight. It was such an up-close and graphic display of nature. And even though most children don't find crickets a particularly endearing insect, it was still a creature that we'd witnessed alive one second and a moment later decapitated and having its head eaten.

"That must be one hungry lizard," Ivy said.

"Can we have dessert?" Emilia asked.

Nana and Papa offered to buy the girls ice cream on their way back to the pousada and keep them overnight in their room so that Mike and I might stay out a bit longer.

The best bars in Arraial d'Ajuda aren't bars in the

traditional sense but cocktail vendors who sell their drinks from carts that serve as traveling bars, much like the food vendors. They line up along the street, with endless bottles of alcohol, fresh fruit, enormous menus detailing their offerings, and small plastic tables and chairs where patrons can linger, though they are also permitted to walk around with drinks in hand. Everywhere we went in Brazil, walking around with alcohol was allowed, and people did not scoff at what hour you might begin your drinking, with groups of old men gathering at ten in the morning for beer at the sidewalk tables of restaurants, much like you might see men gathering at a diner for coffee in the United States. It's an accepted and normal daily ritual.

The next morning, Mike and I were mildly hung over from an excess of caipirinhas. Nonetheless, we gathered with Manoe and Mike's dad in the lobby of the pousada, after saying a brief hello and goodbye to our daughters, who had neither missed nor noticed our absence and were happy to have Nana all to themselves. She agreed to take the girls swimming in the pousada's small pool while the rest of us went on the day's planned activity, which was a three-hour hike along the beach to a neighboring town. Three hours is a significant amount of time to be on a hike, but since the terrain was only beach, without any forests or hills or sand dunes, we weren't concerned.

"I'm sure the kids could do the hike if you wanted them to," Manoe said as we set out. "It's not very hard."

"That's okay," Mike answered. "They're pretty tired. They'll be fine just hanging out with my mom."

After an hour, I reminded myself that activities that are easy for Manoe are often challenging for us mere mortals. The hard-packed beach left us with aching feet and ankles. No amount of sunscreen could protect us from the blazing sun, even though it was still a long way from noon.

"Can you imagine if we'd tried to bring the kids?" I asked Mike.

"There's no way in hell," he said. "We'd be doing two and a half hours of piggyback rides." While we recognize that sometimes there are great benefits to pushing our children, and they often surprise us by rising to the challenge, as they had during many grueling hikes in the Amazon, there are plenty of other times when we're quite sure letting them sit one out is the right call. And the three-hour hike was just such an instance.

The hike ended in the town of Trancoso. While we trekked along the sand, my mother-in-law and daughters had met up with Marcello, who brought them to the beach where our hike ended.

"How was it?" Mike's mom asked.

"I just want a drink," my father-in-law answered. "It was hard." He is a fit and active man, but aching feet and the blazing sun had done us all in.

"Do you have a waiter?" I asked.

"Not yet," my mother-in-law answered.

"You're at a restaurant on the beach and you don't have a drink?"

"I know," she said. "It feels very wrong. We haven't been here that long. The girls have only been playing in the water for a few minutes." Emilia and Ivy jumped at the water's edge, shrieking with every approach of a miniscule wave and running up the beach away from it, before it receded and they chased it back to sea.

We waited so long that we'd just decided to go when a waiter approached. But by then we'd packed up our stuff and agreed to move on. This is rare for me, as I have endless patience when it means I'll get a drink if I hold out long enough.

"Wait, maybe we should stay and have lunch here," Mike said.

"We've been waiting forever. I just think we should move on from here. Why don't we go back to Arraial d'Ajuda and have lunch there? We haven't checked out the beach there yet," I countered. Our experience in Arraial d'Ajuda had been limited to the food and drink vendors and wishing ribbons.

We looked to Mike's parents. His dad shrugged, and his mom said, "We're totally fine with whatever you want to do. You guys decide."

"I just feel like if we go, we're going to end up spending the rest of the day back at the hostel sitting around a crappy pool," Mike said. "It physically pains me to leave the beach."

"Look at me," I commanded. "I promise you we will not end up back at the hostel sitting around a crappy pool. I promise you. I will not let that happen."

We piled into the van, and I was grateful that the tour company hadn't planned for us to make the return hike. Manoe might have suggested such a thing, had incoming tides not prohibited the walk back, submerging a narrow stretch of the journey and turning it from beach to sea.

On some of the long drives, Marcello played a Disney movie in English on a small monitor that sat above the driver's seat.

"He wants to know if you want him to put a movie on for the kids now," Manoe translated.

"That's okay," Mike answered. "We want to save the

movies to break up the really long, seven-hour rides when we're covering a lot of ground."

Manoe relayed the information that a movie wouldn't be necessary, but Marcello still fiddled at the console, and the screen above the cab, viewable only to us passengers, came to life. We watched a montage of American music videos from the 80s, 90s, and early 2000s. And I realized, while watching Axl Rose make out with a supermodel, that the music video revolution had been a new way to introduce mild porn to children. Britney Spears sang "I'm Not a Girl, Not Yet a Woman" with a cross around her neck, dangling just above her boobs, which threatened to break free at any moment.

When the driver pulled up to the hostel, Ivy was exhausted. "Can't we just take a rest?" she asked. Mike shot me a look.

"Yeah," Emilia chimed in. "Ivy and Mom can take a rest, and Dad and I can go into the pool!" She gestured to the crappy pool that Mike dreaded, where she and Ivy had spent the morning frolicking with Nana. It wasn't that the pool was overly crappy, but Mike will rarely choose a pool when there is a beach within walking distance. And if he is going to hang out at a pool, he wants it to be one where there is a staff there to bring you drinks. This pool was more the type where backpackers sat on the edge and cooled off worn feet.

"No, Ivy. We're going to the beach to have some lunch," I said. "And you might even get a treat." Her shoulders still slumped. "And I'll give you a piggyback ride!"

We walked through town and down a steep hill, during which Ivy grudgingly had to get off of my back and walk. Cars zoomed by in the opposite direction. A light rain began to fall. No one mentioned it. We all pretended it wasn't happening and forged ahead to the beach. When we reached the beach, it was pouring, and as crowds departed, ours was the only group heading toward the water in the increasing rainstorm. We found a covered table at a restaurant on the beach, and a waiter practically ran to us to take our order, the opposite of the restaurant in Trancoso.

"What do you want?" I asked Mike.

"I wonder if they do piña coladas."

"They do! It's right here on the menu." I ordered piña coladas for Mike and myself, caipivodkas for the in-laws, and Guaraná, a Brazilian soft drink, for the kids. The drinks arrived, the skies cleared, and the sun returned. A woman with a guitar set up nearby to provide entertainment. We ordered fries and fish for the kids and two orders of *moqueca* with shrimp for the adults. Moqueca is another dish that Bahia is known for, a seafood stew of sorts served over rice. It was excellent, and the waiter continued to excel, sprinting to us to take orders and deliver drinks and food.

"This is way too much food," I said.

"Yes, we definitely over-ordered," my father-in-law said. "We could have shared one of these dishes."

"For sure," my mother-in-law added.

Yet, as we chatted about the overabundance of food on the table, we also managed to eat every last bite.

Maybe it was the early morning hangover, the three-mile trek on the beach, or the stress of the sudden storm, but that meal on the beach could not have been more perfect. I hadn't liked getting caught in the rain, but the piña coladas made up for it.

* * *

The Chocolate Factory

I think being a mother helps keep your feet on the ground. There's very little dignity in parenthood. It's a great leveler.

—Frances O'Grady

Obtaining cash in big cities in Brazil had been difficult, but in the small towns like Arraial d'Ajuda, it was impossible. We were low on cash and needed to replenish. The occasional ATMs we found wouldn't accept our cards, were out of money, or disconnected from a power source and therefore useless. We could use credit cards in stores and restaurants but felt the impact of thin wallets as we passed by the street vendors set up with their outdoor bars.

"Go ask them if they take cards," Mike suggested.

"Okay, but it's a long shot." I approached a woman from whom we'd purchased drinks on our first night in town and asked in Portuguese if she accepted credit cards.

"No," she answered. "But it's okay. Just order what you want and you can come and pay me tomorrow."

Her offer struck me as unique on many levels. There was the basic trust in the fact that we would be honest and return to make good on a debt. Also, she was assuming that by the following night, we would have acquired cash, but I had no reason to believe that of all the defunct cash machines we'd located, one would miraculously be in working order the next day. In any case, I informed her that we couldn't, as we'd be leaving early the next morning, but I thanked her for the kind offer.

The next morning, we hit the road, passing more shacks, and I couldn't help but wonder what life inside them was like. We drove by jungles where the plants seemed woven into one another, where no tree stood solitary but all reached out to their neighbors. We passed an eighteen-wheeler parked along the side of the road. The trucker and his wife and kids sat at a folding table parked next to the rig, having lunch, and again I marveled at the diversity of family life and experiences on our planet.

"Our first stop will be for chocolate," Manoe said. "This region is famous for cocoa. And I really think you'll like it."

Chocolate da Bezinha along the BR101 was a stand more than a store, a small structure where one could purchase chocolates, attached to the farm where the cocoa plants grew. The crops were surrounded by intimidating layers of fencing and barbed wire, and Manoe explained that this was necessary to keep others from harvesting the farmer's crops. We were first offered a sample, and it was delicious, though nothing like the chocolate we think of when we consider Hershey's. It was more textured, like a lighter version of fudge, and came in chocolate, chocolate and coffee, chocolate and banana, and chocolate with coconut. We purchased small plastic tubs of it for so little money that for the longest time I thought I was mishearing the man when he told me the total I owed.

"Mom, look at this!" Emilia said. She pointed to the ground where a grasshopper lay, flattened by tires or feet or both. Except it was about six inches long, the largest grasshopper I'd ever seen.

"There's one over here, too," Ivy said.

As unique as the grasshoppers were, and taking into consideration that I have no great fear of grasshoppers, nor do I wish them any ill will, I was glad that they were dead. It's one thing to have insects hopping and flying around but quite another thing to have six-inch insects buzzing by.

The vendor of Chocolate da Bezinha handed out promotional material in the form of calendars before bidding us farewell.

"So I guess Fridays are for sex?" Mike whispered to me as we walked back to the van.

"What the hell are you talking about?" I countered. He motioned to the calendar, where the abbreviation for Friday, *Sexta-feira*, which literally translates to "sixth market" was Sex. "Well, I don't know that we need to restrict it to Fridays, but yes, it seems like a good way to cap off the week."

"Maybe one day we'll have our own bedroom again," he said.

"Yeah," I agreed. "It will have a door we can close and everything!"

"What are you talking about?" Emilia asked.

"Nothing. Have some more chocolate," I said as we buckled into our seats.

"Our next stop will be where they grow and make açaí," said Manoe, then smiled at the girls. "You're going to get a lot of treats today." Ivy beamed, as if all her wishes were coming true.

One of the first phrases I'd learned when studying Portuguese, along with *pão de queijo*, the cheese buns that were quite tasty when purchased anywhere other than the Londrina airport, was *açaí na tigela*, which literally means "açaí in the bowl." It's a popular Brazilian treat, is considered healthy, and is widely available. We reached the stop, another small storefront attached to the much larger area of açaí crops and production, and I ordered one large *açaí na tigela* with granola and bananas for Mike and me to share with the girls at a small, plastic table. My in-laws ordered their own and sat on the other side of the patio. We ate and enjoyed the shade as well as a break from the van.

After fighting our kids for a share of the treat, which they were reluctant to give up, we let them devour every last little speck. Manoe approached then and asked if we were ready to get back in the van. We nodded, and she turned to pose the question to my father-in-law.

He looked sheepish. "We just ordered another one."

"*Another* bowl of açaí?" she asked with surprise.

"Yes," he confirmed.

"Oh, okay. Just let us know when you're ready."

Back on the road, we passed men standing along the street selling long strings of dried, salted shrimp. "Bahia is known for these," Manoe said. And I realized that of all the states we'd visited, none had so many things it was "known" for as Bahia.

"At our next stop," she added, "we're going to take a tour of a chocolate factory." Ivy squealed with delight.

During most of our van travels, I kept my nose pressed to the glass, not wanting to miss any of the landscape and snapshots of rural Brazilian life. We traveled through what was undoubtedly a poor town, evidenced by more shacks and decay, crumbling concrete, and exposed wires and rebar. As we drove slowly along a road, we caught a glimpse of four teenagers being detained by policemen. All of the teenagers wore board shorts and were shirtless and barefoot. One appeared to be showing documents or identification to a policeman, while the other three stood with their backs to the road, feet spread, with their hands on the backs of their heads. They were very still and obedient, and I noted a second policeman standing next to them, his giant gun raised, no doubt to inspire just such obedience. The place seemed sad. And a minute later, the van pulled over. Whatever was happening with the police and teenagers was taking place a stone's throw from our destination.

The Ilhéus Chocolate Factory had ceased giving tours, so we instead mingled in the shop and indulged in yet more treats. Chocolate liqueur and mixes for hot cocoa were for sale, and a large case displayed a variety of truffles and other chocolate items. We sampled spicy truffles, chocolate-covered cherries, and white chocolate truffles with almonds while the girls gravitated to the more familiar chocolate with puffed rice, the Brazilian equivalent of a Crunch bar. As soon as we'd finished, Ivy told me she needed to go to the bathroom.

"Me, too," said Emilia. The other adults were milling around, looking at the offerings, and occasionally ordering one more.

"Mike," I called, "I'm just going to take the girls to the bathroom."

We walked down a narrow hallway where a bathroom held a single stall. From the expressions on my daughters' faces alone, I knew that we were in for more than just a quick pee. After Ivy went, I flushed for her while she washed her hands, and Emilia took her turn. When she was done with her considerable business, the toilet tank hadn't yet filled back up. I waited a second, while Emilia washed her hands, and then attempted to flush. But the toilet was only capable of a mediocre attempt at clearing the bowl. The evidence of our visit remained.

"Mom, can we go now?" Emilia asked.

"Not yet. We just need to wait another minute." I waited until I thought the toilet tank might have had enough time to fill up and again attempted to flush. The situation did not improve. The girls grew restless. "You know what, you girls go ahead on out there. I'll be out in a minute." They walked back out to the lobby and met up with the rest of the group.

I waited.

It has to be ready by now, I thought. I felt I'd waited longer than my previous attempts and was sure that this time the toilet would flush. But if it didn't, I'd be delaying the clearing of the bowl even longer. And surely people were beginning to worry. *It has to be ready by now.* The toilet was still running, but I made my decision and again attempted to flush, then watched as my daughter's giant poo drifted tauntingly in a lazy circle around the bowl.

"Oh, screw it," I said. As much as I hated to leave a facility's bathroom with such evidence behind, I didn't know what else to do. We hadn't *broken* the toilet, I reasoned. I resigned myself to the situation and walked out of the bathroom and down the hall to the lobby. Apparently everyone in our group had grown tired of waiting for *me* to finish in the bathroom. The lobby was completely deserted except for the two women working behind the counter, who eyed me as I headed straight for the exit. I took solace in knowing that I would never see those women again. I would take responsibility for the poo we left behind, because sometimes that's what motherhood comes down to. You take one for the team.

* * *

Capoeira Etiquette

I feel like with sport, you're playing games. But with exercise, you're literally just trying to stop yourself from dying too young. It's weird.

—James McAvoy

Three towns prior, I'd noted that the hostels and pousadas we'd stayed in got nicer as the trip progressed. That thought seemed like a jinx as we pulled into the final stay of our coastal tour with Manoe. From the exterior, the hostel was beautiful, a striking green building trimmed in white, four floors high, with antique shutters and surrounded by manicured lawns. It was a nice hostel, even an historic hostel, but also one without air-conditioning. This was the first place without some form of air-conditioning since staying in the jungle, but in the jungle it got cold at night, so even without climate control, we were afforded a respite from the heat. Not so in Itacaré.

We were shown to our room. In the past, that would imply the room where Mike, our daughters, and I would sleep. But space was at a premium here, and the only room for us was a true hostel room, a small square of space with two triple-decker bunk beds. With beds for six people, it was time to get comfy with the in-laws.

No one was excited about hanging out in our stifling room for very long, so we walked to a nearby bar and restaurant to have a drink. Manoe and Marcello (who had to share different rooms with other hostel guests) would meet us there after an hour's time, and then the eight of us would venture into town to a restaurant Marcello recommended.

"Well, this is nice," my mother-in-law said as we sat at an outdoor table, having just ordered a round of drinks.

"I think the sky is about to throw up on us," Ivy said. She was correct. The sky darkened, giving brief warning before it began to pour. All of the outdoor patrons scurried to the inside portion of the restaurant, and we were fortunate to get a table in the back. We ordered fries to tide over the girls and sipped on our drinks. A television monitor sat nearby. My in-laws and I couldn't see the screen from our vantage point, but Mike and the girls could, and the three of them quickly lost any ability to maintain conversation.

"What are they watching?" I asked my father-in-law. He craned his neck to see.

"It looks like some sort of *Star Wars*."

Manoe and Marcello arrived, and as the eight of us ventured into town, Mike confided in me that it appeared to be a pirated copy of the latest *Star Wars* movie, one that had been released in theaters after we'd left America, and therefore one that we'd never seen. "And now I really want to see it," he added.

"Unfortunately, I don't think that's going to happen while we're in Brazil."

He didn't answer, but our dinner conversation continued to revolve around movies.

"Have you seen *How to Train Your Dragon 2?*" Emilia asked Nana.

"No," she said. "Is it good? I think I've only seen *How to Kill Your Dragon* but not *How to Kill Your Dragon 2.*"

"*Train*, Nana," I whispered. "*How to* Train *Your Dragon.* You don't want to the kill the dragon. The dragon's a good guy."

"Shit, thanks," she whispered back.

Because of the oppressive heat in the building, we got little sleep that night, and when we emerged from our room the next morning, one by one in the hopes of stealthily sneaking into one of the hostel's bathrooms to use the facilities and brush teeth, we found dozens of Brazilian children in the common area outside of our door. There was a busload of school kids staying in the hostel with us, which accounted for the lack of space. It was their final stay at the hostel, though, and after breakfast, the children boarded their school bus and left. They were replaced by a group of young adult backpackers who arrived later that afternoon. When the school bus had departed and the common room emptied out, Manoe joined us with her laptop.

"So, later today we'll do a capoeira class and then get to watch an exhibition of it tonight. My husband does capoeira, so I wanted to show you a bit of what it's like." She pulled up a video of her husband, a tall, fit Brazilian, and we watched the display of half dance, half martial arts, during which participants stand on their hands, spin on their heads, flip in the air, and execute dozens of other moves that defy gravity and what I'd come to think of as the basic limitations of the human body. "This was at his belt ceremony, so they did some of it with weapons." She showed us another video of competitors using knives in an impressive show of athleticism and grace, during which thankfully no blood was shed.

"That looks so cool," said Mike.

"Yeah," I agreed. "I can't wait to do the capoeira class tonight."

"Okay, well right now we are going to go on another hike. This one goes both on the beach and through a little bit of jungle. Are you ready?"

We groaned.

"What?! You don't want to go?"

"We just hiked three hours on a beach the other day," my father-in-law said. "If the rest of you want to go, that's fine, but I need a break."

"But what about the jungle?" Manoe asked. "Don't you want to do a little jungle hike?"

"Before you picked us up in Rio, we spent a week doing hikes in the Amazon," I explained.

"Nobody got very much sleep last night," Mike added. "So I think we're just going to sit this one out. Especially if you want us to make the capoeira class and the exhibition tonight."

"Okay," Manoe said, and I wondered if she thought us soft.

With so much activity over the previous few weeks, Mike and I had little time for actual work and felt the pressure mounting of unanswered e-mails and tasks fallen by the wayside. Nana and Papa agreed to take Emilia and Ivy to the beach. Mike and I would get a few hours of work done, then walk down to meet them at lunchtime. When we arrived at the beach, everyone was ready for lunch. There were beachside restaurants, but my in-laws had been at the beach all morning and wanted to venture into town instead and do a little shopping. We bade them farewell, took over the childcare duties, and had lunch on the beach while the girls played.

"Did you see Emilia's shoulders?" I asked Mike.

"Yes, she's looking awfully pink. Did we not bring sunscreen?"

We'd liberally applied sunscreen that morning, but hours of playing in the water had gone by, and they needed another dose.

"No, I don't have any on me," I said.

"I'll see if I can go find some. Order me another drink, will you?"

Mike wandered off down the beach in search of a vendor who might sell sunscreen. I ordered a round of drinks and made the girls take a break from playing for a hasty few minutes of eating when the food arrived. Mike returned ten minutes later with an empty bottle of sunscreen that had been neatly cleaved in half.

"This was the best I could do," he said. "It was in a trash can at a board rental shop. The guy took a knife and cut it open." With the bottle cut in half, we could reach the remnants of sunscreen, which were plentiful, that you couldn't access otherwise.

"That's so MacGyver of you," I said.

After another hour on the beach, we gathered the girls to walk back to the hostel.

"Why do we have to go back?" Emilia asked.

"Because we have a big night tonight, and it's best if we all go take a rest now so we have lots of energy for the caipirinha class."

"We're going to make the drinks again?" Ivy asked.

"Oh, I meant the capoeira class," I said. I saw Mike smirking, reveling in the fact that I misspoke, as I'm usually the one pointing out the linguistic mishaps he and his parents make.

"Have another drink," he said.

"Mom," Emilia said, "I'm afraid I won't be able to do it. I don't know how."

"Don't worry, honey, that's why we're going to do a class." She was naturally intimidated by the video Manoe had shown us of seasoned capoeira practitioners. "We won't be doing the hard stuff. We'll just learn some of the basic moves."

"But you know what would be cool?" she continued. "If when I got back to school I could show my friends how I can spin on my head." Emilia often has an odd mix of intimidation and overconfidence, and I didn't correct her thinking that by the end of the evening she might be able to spin on her head.

"Mom?" Ivy asked. "Do I *have* to have a knife?" Clearly what remained in Ivy's mind was the demonstration of knife play.

"No, Ivy. No one is going to have any knives, I promise."

"Oh, good," she said. And I realized that I'd done a poor job of explaining what I expected the capoeira class to be. The video Manoe had shown us had put fantastical ideas into my daughters' minds.

We reached the hostel, and I helped the girls shower before putting them down for a nap. We had to wake them after a few hours, despite the fact that they wanted to sleep longer, because Manoe didn't want us to be late for the class. When they woke, dressing them was a dilemma, as there were no clean clothes in sight. And once again I went with the method of selecting the least offensive articles of clothing we had.

"Just go without underwear," I instructed Ivy.

"Whoa, really?" she asked with wide eyes, as if this were truly a special treat.

"It's just a short walk to a beach where we'll meet the capoeira instructor," Manoe said as we set out from the hostel.

My husband, in-laws, and I all looked at each other with expressions of doubt. Manoe would describe a half marathon as "a short walk."

The beach was a small but lively area shielded on one side by a rocky outcropping. Palms dotted the area, and one stand served as a bar, and another sold fresh fruit.

"I'll just go and find the instructor," Manoe said, looking around, concerned.

The rest of us sat on a grassy slope, people-watching.

"I have no problem with this view," my mother-in-law said. It seemed an odd statement. The beach was nice but certainly not the most impressive of all the beaches we'd seen. Then I realized what she was looking at, a group of shirtless and physically perfect twenty-something men tossing a ball back and forth.

We spent ten minutes watching a man practicing on a tightrope suspended a few feet off the ground, tied between two palm trees. And I decided I wanted one. We'd put it in the backyard, and I'd practice and perfect my balance, of which I am lacking, and in doing so, I'd develop tremendous core strength. I'd have *abs*. Note: this never actually happened.

"I'm so sorry, guys," Manoe said, returning to our group. "I don't know where the instructor is. It's really not like him, but it looks like there's not going to be a class."

"That's okay," I said. As much as I'd been looking forward to the class, I was secretly relieved that I was being spared what was sure to be an embarrassing endeavor.

"Can I buy you all a drink to make up for it? I feel so bad, especially since this is the last full day of your tour."

Manoe bought the girls sodas and the adults caipirinhas. I bought a giant slice of watermelon from the fresh fruit stand for Ivy.

We walked to town and agreed to find a restaurant. We'd have dinner and kill time before the capoeira exhibition that would take place that evening. At dinner, Manoe ordered penne with pesto. It was an unexpected order from someone who appeared so healthy, in every aspect of the word, and I was sure she didn't typically order pasta. But when it arrived, she ate only a few bites, despite the admission that it was excellent, and I realized that if you excel at portion control, you can enjoy a greater number of foods without negatively affecting your health and your waistline. I do not excel at portion control.

When it was time to go to the capoeira exhibition, we made our way to a building with an open-air patio area in the back. The capoeira master was there, an ancient, wiry man with a cane. Because he hadn't shown up for the class, for which we never learned the reason, he offered to give us a brief class before the scheduled event. He was shadowed by five children, between the ages of eight and twelve. He told them what to do while Manoe translated, and we attempted to mirror their movements. It began as a simple stepping motion, a swaying fighting stance as one arm swings forward and one leg swings back. The motion, called the *ginga*, is repeated, back and forth. I know that it was a simple move, but suddenly I couldn't tell left from right, and no matter how many times I tried to correct myself, I was always blatantly off from the rest of the group. This is the same reason I don't participate in things like Zumba or line dancing. Ivy may have inherited this from me, as she was in tears after only a few minutes. I decided that she and I would cut our losses, and I pulled her over to a bench where she sat on my lap as we watched the others. My father-in-law was seated from the start, though Mike, my mother-in-law, and Emilia all participated.

My father-in-law leaned over to me and said, "My hips don't move that way."

After some basic instruction (though not basic enough for Ivy or me), the master had those participating all sit in a circle. The children sang and kept the beat unless they were engaging. Two people would face each other, one from our group and one of the children, and they would do a mock version of the art. When it was Emilia's turn, she looked at me as if to say, "I don't know what I'm supposed to do." But instead of bailing, she went with it, doing her best to mirror her opponent, a young boy of a similar age. All of the children who were well versed in capoeira showed patience and understanding with the foreign newbies. Mike and my mother-in-law both did well with their few minutes in the center of the circle, and when Manoe faced off, it was clear to us that she'd been studying it herself for some time. People started to trickle in, both spectators and capoeiristas. It was obvious when some of them showed up, as they walked in with fat-free physiques and toned muscles. Before we knew it, the place was packed with men and women of all ages. The circle widened, and it appeared Ivy and I had lucked out when we'd taken our seat, as we had a direct view of the action.

Across the circle from us was the starting point for the capoeiristas taking their turn. Behind them stood the musicians, anchored by those playing the *berimbau*, a single-stringed bow and percussive instrument. It resembles a large bow with what looks like a gourd at the bottom. Other instruments include the *pandeiro*, similar to a tambourine, *atabaques*, large standing drums, an *agogô* bell, and a *ganzá*, a handheld percussive cylinder with contents that make a satisfying rattle when shaken. The instruments, along with call-and-answer songs, keep the beat and determine the tempo of the capoe-iristas' movements.

The capoeiristas crouched low in two lines that met in front of the musicians. I watched them waiting for their turns and realized that the mere thought of this, the resting position, hurt my knees. Those at the front of each line faced off against one another, though competitors could move to the front of the line if they wanted to go against a certain individual, and this happened often and was accepted. Competitors touched hands, then moved in a half-cartwheel motion before taking the fighting stance in the middle of the arena. Inexperienced practitioners would move in slow motion at times, and the martial arts aspect of capoeira occurs without physically touching your opponent. They come close to kicking each other in the head, but the art is in doing so without contact.

When the experienced capoeiristas took center stage, the real show began. There were backflips and balancing on one arm and so many instances in which I was sure I was about to see someone's head split open. We watched for two hours. There were countless times when a foot swiped the air so close to us that I feared Ivy's nose would get broken. A spray of sweat hit us in the face. In the midst of the unbelievable displays of athleticism, a two-year-old took his turn, facing off against a four-year-old who balanced on his head at one point. After we passed the two-hour mark, I nudged Mike. He, Emilia, Manoe, and my mother-in-law had moved to the spectators' circle when the big boys had shown up. Ivy was covered in sweat, sprawled on my lap.

"This is awesome," I said to Mike, "but I don't know how long it's going to go for." It seemed the event could continue deep into the night.

"Yeah, we should go," Mike whispered back. "This one's sweaty and tired," he said, motioning to Emilia on his lap.

"This one, too," I said. Looking down at Ivy in her soaked T-shirt and skirt, something occurred to me. "Wait, are you wearing a skirt?" I asked her.

"Yes," she said. "This is what you told me to wear."

"This is a skirt? It doesn't have shorts underneath?"

"No, it's a skirt," she confirmed.

"But you're not wearing any underwear."

"Because you *told* me not to wear any underwear," she said, exasperated that she now appeared to be in trouble for following directions.

"I know, I know. It's not your fault. I mean, I'm not mad. It's just . . ." I was pretty sure we'd unintentionally flashed the musicians and competitors at least once in the preceding two hours. "Yeah, we should really go."

The hostel was quieter that night, the busload of Brazilian kids having departed and been replaced by the notably serene group of twenty-something men. The breeze from the night before had gone, and the air in our room was stifling. Sleep was an impossibility. Unless you were a six- or eight-year-old. My daughters had no trouble sleeping peacefully through the night. The rest of us spent the night falling asleep but waking after only ten minutes because it was simply too hot, and our bodies would alert us in alarm.

Sometime after midnight, I got up to pee. I cracked open the door to our room to find the common area outside our door filled with the twenty-somethings. They were sleeping, fully clothed, directly on the wood floor, their hands folded neatly as if in repose. I quietly walked in between them to make it to the bathroom. I could only assume that their room was too hot, and sleeping on the floor in the common area was a more comfortable option. When I returned to our room, I saw that Mike had given up trying to sleep and instead was typing away on his laptop while sitting up in his bunk. I resorted to reading.

My in-laws appeared to sleep on and off, but rather than suffer the whopping eighteen inches of separation between their two bunks, they crawled into one bunk together. It was both adorable and baffling, as I couldn't imagine adding another's body heat to the already stifling surroundings. If my kids had woken from nightmares, I would have comforted them with words and reassuring pats at arm's length. Perhaps that seemed heartless, but after my failure in even dressing my daughter appropriately, I'd long since given up on a stellar day in my role as mom.

* * *

Morning Call

I love the idea of waking up to a song. It could be any song.
—Shreya Ghoshal

The last long drive to Salvador didn't include highways but instead took us through small towns on cobblestoned roads, over mammoth speed bumps, and through endless poverty. We passed Mototaxi stations, where motorcycle drivers worked as taxis, though limited to single passengers at a time. The topography changed to rolling hillsides, and we knew we were in orange country as evidenced by countless vendors of oranges and *suco de laranja*.

"I'm so glad we're here," said Emilia when it was evident we'd reached the city.

"That was a really long drive," Ivy agreed.

"You can say that again," said Nana.

So Ivy dutifully repeated, "That was a really long drive."

But forty minutes later, we were still in Salvador yet not at our destination. At one point we were deterred by a film crew that had blocked access to particular streets. Marcello was more than competent as a driver and took his job very seriously. We were ever grateful that we had him to navigate the narrow streets and save us from trying to do it ourselves. As time went on and we continued to circle the same few streets with no luck in locating the address we were destined for, Marcello and Manoe began speaking in Portuguese, and the little that I picked up made them sound like an old married couple arguing about their inability to find the place. Marcello wanted to continue stopping and hollering out to people on the street for information. Manoe wanted to get out, walk around, and find the place herself. She prevailed and eventually located the building, and Marcello surely wasn't happy about it. This was compounded by Manoe's added rant, an equivalent of I-told-you-so in Portuguese, when she'd have done better to drop the matter. We had a brief farewell with thanks for all of their efforts in the preceding 1,200 miles. After they dropped us off, I'm sure it was a tense ride.

We checked into an odd building, which seemed to be half hotel and half apartments, thus our apartment came with the benefit of a doorman. He welcomed and directed us to an apartment Mike had booked online.

When the six of us walked in, we couldn't believe our luck.

"This place is awesome," my father-in-law said.

"Wow," my mother-in-law echoed. "This is quite the venue!"

Venue is one of her favorite words and she uses it correctly about 50 percent of the time. We'd stayed in some rough accommodations since leaving Londrina, and the apartment in Salvador felt luxurious. There was a master suite, separated by a hallway from a large room with four beds, a kitchen, dining table, and access to a deck with a small cooling pool, about the size of a hot tub, and an incredible view looking out over the water.

"Good job, Mike," I said. "This place is fantastic."

"We'll take the big room with the kids if you two want the master suite," my mother-in-law offered. They'd had the master suite during our time on the riverboat and now offered us the better bedroom in return. My father-in-law cast his eyes down, willing to go with the flow, though I'm sure he'd rather have had more privacy.

We agreed and began settling in, looking forward to the next few days of being in one place and in relative comfort after so many days on the road. But something seemed off. I walked into our bedroom, then back out to the larger room. I looked around. The kitchen was large. The deck was large. There were plenty of sleeping spaces. I walked back into our bedroom and peered into the bathroom. Then again went to the larger room.

"There's only one bathroom," I announced.

"What?" Mike looked up.

We'd all shared a bathroom before, and in many hostels we'd shared bathrooms with dozens of strangers, but those bathrooms had been accessible to all.

"There's only one bathroom, and it's in our bedroom," I said. "So anyone using the bathroom has to walk through our bedroom to get to it."

Suddenly, the place was a notch less fabulous than it had been a moment before. Having the master bedroom wasn't as special when you considered that four other humans would be trudging through it any time they wanted to use the bathroom. And the four other humans were less than thrilled about going into someone else's bedroom to get to a toilet.

That evening, before heading out for dinner, my in-laws began ironing their clothes.

"How do you guys still have clean clothes?" I asked, bewildered. "I feel like if I ironed any of my clothes, I'd just be baking the dirt right in."

The streets of our neighborhood in Salvador's historic Pelourinho district looked menacing in daylight. But as night approached, the dilapidated buildings took on an old world charm. We'd arrived on a Tuesday evening, and as it happens, every Tuesday Pelourinho throws a Big-Ass Party (not the official term). Of course, this started as a weekly religious service, and the religious aspects of the tradition still take place, but most of the neighborhood is engaged in the Big-Ass Party. There are capoeira exhibitions, barbecues, and street bars. Whichever church you pray at or whatever aspect of the party you engage in, you'll do so to a background of drumming. Drum corps large and small march through the city with deep, fast beats, and I couldn't help but feel the music in my chest, like a secondary heartbeat.

Early the next morning, my mother-in-law snuck in, as was expected, to use the restroom. My father-in-law took his turn a few minutes later. Mike and I feigned continued sleep to take any awkwardness out of the arrangement, but I watched through slitted eyes as my father-in-law crept into our room, into the bathroom, and then *almost* closed the door all the way before his morning pee. My father-in-law is legendary for his inability to close doors, thus my husband and I woke fully to the sounds of his father's morning urination.

I spent much of the morning doing laundry, or as close as I could come to doing laundry, in a bucket in the bathroom. Hand washing clothes is a necessary skill for anyone on long-term travel where washing machines aren't readily available, and anyone in this position knows that washing clothes isn't that difficult, but drying them is. Denim and socks dry into hard items that need to be massaged into pliability, and more often than not, you end up having to pack damp clothing that hasn't dried by the time you need to leave for your next destination. I still felt the need to try.

I was looking forward to spending our last evening in Salvador with my in-laws, who would leave Brazil the same time that we would head back to Londrina, the city of our home exchange. But after doing laundry, I felt exhausted and had to lie down. After an hour, I realized that I wasn't tired. I was achy.

When I walked out to the big room to check on the others, my father-in-law was curled up on his bed in the fetal position. "He's nauseous," my mother-in-law whispered.

Ivy and Emilia looked at books on their bed, but Emilia looked up at me and said, "Mom, my stomach hurts."

"I'll take care of her," Mike interjected, looking up from his laptop. "Why don't you go lie down again. You don't look so good."

I returned to the bedroom, and despite the heat of Brazil, turned off our precious air-conditioning and bundled up in bed to calm feverish shivering. After hours of rest and a handful of pills that I hoped were intended to treat whatever ailed me, I rallied. We planned to go to a restaurant right across the street. At the last minute, my father-in-law decided that instead of dinner, he needed more time curled up in the fetal position. We left him to rest and went out.

The restaurant was charming, almost cave-like with low lighting and walls of stone. We ordered, and as we waited for our drinks and food to arrive, Emilia's body slumped lower in her chair, as if oozing down under the force of gravity.

"Are you okay?" Mike asked.

"I want to go back to the apartment," she said.

"Emilia, we haven't even eaten yet," I said.

"I just want to go back."

"I'll tell you what," said Mike. "If you stay and have dinner, we'll order dessert."

"I want to go back," she said again.

With my father-in-law back at the apartment, which was right across the street, this was an option. And with the admission that she'd rather go back than stay for dessert, we knew she truly wasn't feeling well. Mike took her back to the apartment and tucked her into bed before returning to join us at the restaurant.

"So, Mom," Ivy said. "I need to know how you make macaroni and cheese." I'm no Martha Stewart; she referred to the Kraft variety.

"Oh. Uh, okay." I proceeded to outline the steps of boiling water and so forth.

"Okay, how about chili. I need to know how to make chili."

For twenty minutes, Ivy asked questions about recipes she suddenly needed to know. I was vaguely aware that during this time, Mike and his mother were having a dinner table discussion of diarrhea, which Mike's family has never been shy about discussing. And I was thankful that there were few customers and that those present seemed oblivious to our language.

The waitress, who may also have been the owner, was a pleasant woman who chatted with me when I had a rare break in the action from Ivy. She spoke only Portuguese, so the conversation took considerable effort, and I may or may not have understood what she was saying. I thought she was telling me about her children, what they studied and where they worked. In any case, I nodded and smiled dumbly, hoping this was an appropriate response.

As we left the restaurant, she showed us the fish tank, which was more of a small pool of water in a hollowed-out hearth. A lone, small fish swam, visible under a nearby blue lightbulb. It was an odd scene, and at the same time the fish looked like he belonged there.

In the middle of the night, we were woken by Emilia's sudden need for the bathroom. She suffered vomiting and diarrhea, and I felt a pang of guilt for having tried to bait her with dessert into staying at the restaurant when she was obviously hurting.

In the morning, we packed, and the doorman called us a cab to take us to the airport. There was a long line to check in, and when we finally had our boarding passes, I herded everyone quickly to the security check area.

"I'd really like to stop and look for some Alka-Seltzer," my father-in-law said. But we whizzed by shops that might have had such remedies; I was afraid the security line would be as long as the check-in line, which would put us in danger of missing our flight.

"I'm hungry," Mike added.

"Let's just get through security," I said. "I'm sure you can get all of those things on the other side."

My rushing was in vain, as security was very fast. Not once in all our travels in Brazil did I take off shoes or belt, remove my laptop, or display liquids.

"Where's Papa?" Ivy asked.

"Papa always has to go through extra security," Nana explained. Sure enough, my father-in-law had been pulled aside and was getting an additional inspection. "Because he has a metal hip."

"Wow," said Emilia. "He's like Ironman."

On the other side of security, guilt weighed upon me, as there was plenty of food but none of the shops with medicine that I'd hurried my father-in-law past, thereby robbing him of his chance to procure Alka-Seltzer or its Brazilian equivalent.

No one suffered vomiting or diarrhea on our two-and-a-half-hour flight to São Paulo, for which I was grateful, though Emilia continued to feel waves of nausea. In São Paulo, we said goodbye to the in-laws. I was well aware of the fact that not every family could function with basic civility after embarking on such an adventure together, and we're extremely lucky to be three generations who can travel extensively without bickering and arguing along the way. I owe them a debt of gratitude for that. And perhaps a box of Alka-Seltzer.

* * *

Space to Breathe

*What a lovely surprise to finally discover
how unlonely being alone can be.*

—Ellen Burstyn

"Let's see here," said Ivy, sitting in the seat next to me. She opened up the flight safety card and perused it as if it were a menu. It's a ritual my children have adopted at the beginning of every flight.

"Like this, Daddy?" Emilia asked. I looked past Mike to see Emilia, holding a barf bag and miming throwing up in it.

"What is she doing?" I asked Mike.

"Practicing."

Emilia sat straight up as if having a lovely flight, then suddenly pretended to throw up into the bag again, this time with accompanying sound effects.

"Do you think she's really going to throw up?" I asked. We had a one-hour flight to get back to Londrina.

"I don't know," he answered. "But if she does, she feels like she'll be better off if she gets a few practice rounds in."

I'd been carrying a plastic bag around in my pocket since

we'd left Salvador for just such an event. Luckily, neither the plastic bag nor the official barf bag was needed, and we made it back to Londrina without incident.

When we'd first arrived in Londrina, it had seemed so foreign, but now, after visiting wildly different places like Rio and the Amazon, it felt small and common and easy. We learned that we missed a terrible storm by just a few days. Before our arrival, the airport had been closed due to persistent fog, the streets had flooded, and portions of the city had no power. Had some English-speaking neighbors not told us of this, we'd never have known.

The next morning, Emilia threw up scrambled eggs in three successive upheavals. We spent much of the morning cleaning up vomit and doing laundry with the luxury and ease of a working washing machine (far more effective than what I can do with a bucket). The unpleasantness of the former task was overshadowed by my joy at the latter, as the prospect of clean clothes was heavenly.

"Should we go to the store?" Mike asked as we folded clothes free of mud and sand and sweat. "We don't have any food here."

"Or *I* could go to the store," I said. "I could walk up to the close one, and then in twenty minutes you guys could come pick me up."

"Or we could just all go," Mike said.

"Hmm. Or I could go alone."

We rarely separated in Brazil and spent most of our time as a very tight-knit four-person family. This was necessitated by language barriers and unfamiliarity with Brazil itself. It made sense to stick together, for the most part. That said, I was more than capable of walking to the nearby store, and my limited Portuguese was more than any of my family members had. Mike stared at me, waiting for an explanation.

"Do you not want us to come?" he asked.

"I love you and the girls so much it hurts, but I absolutely cannot stand shopping with you," I admitted.

"Oh. Okay, then."

Shopping with my husband and daughters means trying to complete tasks while wrangling my children. And I have very well-behaved children, but the wonders of a store with thousands of products on display is just too much for them. It's too much for Mike, as well, as he's easily distracted by any number of things that we don't want, need, and won't consume. A family shopping trip typically ends up with me ordering one of the kids to stay with Mike and one to stay with me in the hopes of not losing our children and completing the task at hand. This lasts for about thirty seconds before Mike shirks his parental responsibility in favor of studying the most grotesque meat product he can find. We leave without getting what we came for, by which time I'm snapping at my children and shooting daggers at Mike with my eyes. Family shopping should not be a thing.

Twenty minutes later, I walked lazily around the small, nearby grocery store, perusing items at will, crossing off everything on my list, and without being responsible for humans other than myself. It was glorious. Faith No More's rendition of "Easy" played over the store speakers, and life was good.

During our first week back in Londrina, once we felt confident all vomiting was behind us, we were eager to return to a restaurant we'd gone to with Mike's parents where everyone had agreed the steak was the best of the trip. That's quite a statement, considering the massive quantities of meat our party had consumed after a month's travels throughout Brazil. Senhor Zanoni's restaurant was by one of Londrina's lakes and housed under a giant palapa-style roof. The kids liked it because of the playroom, complete with trampoline, ball pit, a coloring station, and nonstop animated movies.

We wandered in and over to one of the better seating options, a large round table near the playroom, as opposed to the long bench-style seating that occupied the center of the open room. I took the girls to the playroom to get them signed in, and when I returned to the table, I found Mike in conversation with a man. Conversation might be a bit of a stretch.

"He's saying something to me, and I have no idea what it is," Mike said.

The man turned to me and began speaking. I think he was saying that for one of the bigger, preferred tables, you had to have at least four people. I told him that we had children and pointed to the playroom. He gestured for us to sit but stayed and spoke to us for another ten minutes. He was very kind, and I picked up on a few words, but the majority of our conversation was lost on me, though I did successfully communicate that we were an American family in Brazil on a home exchange. Before he left, he turned the menu in front of me over and pointed to the restaurant's logo on the back. Next to the restaurant's name was a caricature of Senhor Zanoni, and I realized that we'd been talking to the owner. Or trying to talk to the owner.

We received excellent service that evening, and before we left, Senhor Zanoni returned and presented us with a beautiful book on Londrina, with text in both Portuguese and English.

After dinner, as we left the restaurant, we agreed to take a short walk around the lake before returning to our borrowed house. Dozens of joggers ran in pairs along the paved path.

"These people sure are good at exercising," Emilia said. "I wish I knew how to tell them they're doing a good job."

"I'm not sure how to say good job, but you could say good evening," I said.

"How do you say good evening?"

"*Boa noite*."

"*Boa noite*," she repeated, and spent the next twenty minutes of our walk saying good evening to anyone who would listen, and sometimes shouting it to those who appeared not to hear her first attempt.

"She's like our little ambassador," I said to Mike.

"I know. It's awesome."

As we drove home that evening, Mike and I listened to the girls' discussion of future travel plans in the backseat.

"I want to go to Paris," Ivy said. "I wonder if we can drive there."

"I'm pretty sure we have to fly on a plane," Emilia answered.

"That's okay. I like planes. I like it when we get to watch movies on planes. And I want to see the Eiffel Tower."

"I want to go to the hills of South Dakota to dig up dinosaur bones," Emilia said. "And I want to go to Antarctica so that we can be the first kids there."

"Whenever we go on a plane, you should make sure you have a bag with you, because you threw up a lot lately."

"Don't worry," said Emilia. "I've practiced how to throw up in a bag on a plane a *lot*."

* * *

Playmaster

Play is the highest form of research.
—Albert Einstein

There are a few things you never want to see while sitting on the toilet. A roach flying through the air is one of them. I have no problem doing battle with roaches, and I've dispatched many in my time, especially during our travels. Australia, Mexico, Florida, and Brazil all have roaches of uncomfortable sizes. And no, calling them "palmetto bugs" does not make it any better.

The attitude with which you approach a roach situation has a lot to do with the level of stress it will bring you. For instance, one roach is far better than one hundred. An elderly roach is better than a young, spry one, and day is better than night. On the toilet is a less than desirable circumstance. It seems unfair to be confronted with the prospect of battle with a roach when in such a vulnerable position. I'm unprepared and unable to react. I must continue on with business as usual.

Luckily the roach did not fly at me and instead landed on a section of tile surrounding the bathtub. When I was able, I crept to the sink and grabbed the first thing I could, a bottle of Mike's shaving cream. I approached the beast and showered it. I'm happy to say that shaving cream will eventually result in a roach's demise, but it takes a lot of shaving cream. You have to mire the bug down so it can't keep moving away. This resulted in a two-foot smear of shaving cream across the bathroom wall before I really turned up the pressure and the roach could advance no further.

After my inefficient victory, I headed downstairs and was immediately confronted by Emilia.

"Mom, I wrote a song. Do you want to hear it?"

"Of course I want to hear it."

"Okay, here goes . . .

We all went to the Amazon
Now let's go to a nail salon
We have to get out all the dirt
Oh come on, it won't hurt
I know that you really want to
Just Ivy, me, and you."

"That's great, Emilia. Can Tammy come too?"

"And Tammy too. And Tammy too," she crooned.

I hadn't seen my cousin Tammy in years, and she had come to Londrina to visit us for a week. Tammy was the daughter of missionary parents, and she'd lived in Brazil from the age of eight to twelve. She was still fluent in Portuguese, which was handy, and with her greater knowledge of Brazil, she was able to introduce us to foods we might not have otherwise tried. We learned which brands produced the best hearts of palm, how to cut a dragon fruit, and the various uses of frozen passion fruit pulp.

Our time in the Amazon, walking barefoot through miles of mud, had embedded a unique sort of dirt in our nails. This required more than a good scrubbing. We needed manicures and pedicures, and Tammy loved the idea. We drove to the mall, which I thought was fairly fancy, a chic, modern sprawl, but then realized I've spent so little time in malls over the past decade and I can't say I have any measure of what a normal mall should look like.

Tammy took charge of checking us in at a salon while Mike agreed to browse the mall and meet us after an hour. I'd never had a pedicure where my feet were placed in a bucket as opposed to one of those big massage chairs with a mini foot spa at the bottom. Although the bucket did remind me of one year when Mike took me to an Asian foot spa for our anniversary. We sat side by side with our feet in buckets lined with trash bag liners and filled with water. The masseurs were a husband and wife team. Mike got the wife, and I was stuck with the husband, who reeked of cigarettes. It was an odd foot massage during which I wasn't sure whether to laugh or cry, and Mike abandoned me by spending his entire massage with his eyes closed, so that I couldn't commiserate with him via eye contact. It got worse when my masseur stood over me, put his hands on my thighs, and vigorously shook me forward and back. I wasn't sure if I was being massaged, molested, or if he was attempting to dislocate my hips. Mike, a mere foot away, appeared to suffer no such similar assault. We never went back.

At the nail salon in Brazil, I again felt on my own, as I was separated from Tammy and the girls by a large pillar. On the other hand, I was glad that Emilia and Ivy were in the presence of someone who could translate for them.

My nail tech, unfortunately, spoke English. Not well but enough to insult me on various levels, all under the guise of matronly advice.

"Watch your husband," she warned, as if any smart woman would have her spouse on a tight leash at all times.

"You are Christian, yes? You believe Jesus Christ is Savior, yes?" she asked. And I wished that her English was better or my Portuguese was better so that we could really dive into this and other fun topics, like abortion and genocide and how to react when your nail tech offers offensive advice and asks you questions that are none of her damn business.

* * *

Mike and the girls and I were still exhausted from our travels around Brazil and not yet ready to embark on any major ventures beyond that of a single day trip, so during Tammy's stay, we took a road trip to Salto do Apucaraninha, a waterfall about an hour's drive away. Tammy is a professional photographer, so the drive took a little longer with periodic stops when something caught her eye. We reached the waterfall, and there was a viewing platform, which lent some sense of security while gazing down the falls to where the water crashed violently below.

As amazing as the view was, one can only stare at rushing water for so long, but the idea of driving an hour and a half to stare at a waterfall for fifteen minutes, and then drive another hour and a half back, seemed silly. So we walked to the road where we'd parked and hunted around to see if there was a better vantage point. Mike located it, a narrow trail creeping up through rocks and trees, which opened up onto a large, flat rock and offered a better view of the falls and river below. There was no viewing platform, so we took care to keep ourselves and our children far from the edge. Tammy had fallen behind while fiddling with her camera and its myriad accessories. When she finally reached the rock and the opening, she said, "Wow," and then dropped to her stomach and slowly slithered in inch increments to where we stood.

"What are you doing?" I asked.

"I'm just not real comfortable with heights," she answered, trying to scoot on her belly without damaging her camera, "but I do want to get some good pictures."

With this and other precautionary measures, including my death grip on my children's hands that twice prompted cries of "Mom, you're hurting me," no one plummeted over the falls.

That afternoon, as Mike, Tammy, and I sat on the patio, Emilia announced, "Everybody, *just stay here*." We'd been idly chatting and hadn't planned on going anywhere. "We're going to play Emilia's Calf," she explained. Tammy looked at me expectantly, but I shrugged.

"This must be a new game," Mike agreed. "I haven't heard of this one before."

Emilia returned to the living room where she and Ivy were intent on something, so we remained out on the patio and continued our conversation. After a few minutes, Emilia returned and announced, "Emilia's Calf is now open!"

For a terrifying moment, I thought this was a game of butchery or taxidermy, whereby we would be required to pretend to explore the body cavity of a baby cow. I was about to protest that I didn't want to open a calf, when Ivy took center stage and produced menus for each of us.

"We'll be back in just a moment to take your order," Emilia explained.

"Ah," said Mike. "We're playing Emilia's *Café*."

"Oh thank goodness."

The menus, which accompanied an extensive child's kitchen play set, included items in both Portuguese and English, and the girls would take our orders. The "specials" included such combos as chicken and eggs, and salad with hot dog. When we'd placed our orders, we would look through the windows to the living room where the girls dutifully cooked our imaginary orders, then brought them to us, various plastic food replicas in bowls with miniature pink forks, accompanied by tiny cups from which we pretended to drink cappuccinos and milkshakes.

"We have a real restaurant in mind for tonight," I told Tammy as I ate my imaginary eggplant parmigiana.

"Mom," Emilia interjected, "Emilia's Calf is a real restaurant." After a beleaguered sigh, she said, "I have work to do," and returned to her plastic kitchen.

"So, where are we going tonight?" Tammy asked.

"It was recommended by our exchange partners," I said.

Rodeio, the oldest restaurant in Londrina, was founded in 1966 and is the employer of Senhor Nelson, touted the oldest waiter in Londrina, still working hard at the age of seventy-six. Upon our visit, with Tammy graciously serving as translator, we sadly learned that Senhor Nelson was not there.

"Oh no," I whispered. "Did he die?"

"No, he didn't *die*. He's on vacation," Tammy explained.

"Anyone waiting tables in his seventies surely deserves a vacation," Mike said.

When Tammy's visit came to an end, we were sad to see her go. Not only because it was such a short visit after so many years apart but also because she is family and a genuinely lovely person. And let's be honest, it's wonderful when that happens, because "family" sadly doesn't always guarantee "genuinely lovely person." In Tammy, I had both.

* * *

Going to the mall has not been a regular activity for me since my teenage years. In Boise, Mike and I take great pains to avoid the mall, and voicing the word itself for some reason brings to mind the pain and awkwardness of adolescence, mixed with my irrational guilt at being a member of a society that is hyper-focused on acquiring things. However, the sweltering heat of Brazil, not only outdoors but also in our home (air-conditioning was limited to a few rooms and not present in the main living areas), drove us to the mall on more than one occasion. Giant posters of Johnny Depp, selling a watch or cologne or something else we didn't need, were plastered everywhere. In the photo, he rolled up one sleeve with a half sneer on his face, as if he'd just broken wind and was disgusted with himself for being capable of creating such a smell.

We did plenty of clothes shopping, something abhorred at home but which takes on a new light when the merchandise is a fraction of what we'd normally expect to pay. Mike would stop at Bob's Milkshakes on the pretense of getting the girls a treat in order to indulge in his own love of milkshakes. At one point, we allowed the girls to ride motorized animals that they could steer at will across the shiny floors. Despite their sluggish pace, I still panicked that they'd crash into shoppers or plummet down the escalator. As a result, I darted around them constantly blocking different directions in what might have been my most annoying act of motherhood to date.

We navigated the mall a few times successfully while keeping the kids from viewing something called Playmaster, which looked to be a mini-amusement park. Eventually they spotted it.

"Can we go there?" Emilia asked, eyes wide and hopeful.

The first few times, we said no. This is always the gut reaction, from a fear of hanging around anyplace designed for children, because such places are often annoying to adults. We also default to no because of the expense. If we gave in to every request from our children, we'd be in the poorhouse fast. But in the case of Playmaster, we eventually relented. Everything in Brazil was relatively cheap, and Playmaster was no exception.

Playmaster involved paying for a certain number of tokens the kids could use on rides and games. Unlike what comes to mind when I think of an arcade, it was an enormous place, warehouse reminiscent, so it lacked the claustrophobic feeling I get from a Chuck E. Cheese or a boardwalk amusement park. Instead of real tokens, the credits are added to a card that is then swiped at each of the attractions. The girls played video games and air hockey and took a spin in bumper cars. There was a working roller coaster, on which Mike accompanied the girls. Then I saw a ride I recognized from my youth called the Scrambler. Playmaster didn't assign names to its rides, and even if they did, I wouldn't have been able to decipher them; my Portuguese didn't go too far beyond basic pleasantries and numbers.

We hadn't seen anyone on the ride (we had Playmaster largely to ourselves), but I recalled the spider-like contraption with individual buckets at the end of long legs sprouting from the ride's center. These then turned around in circles while the legs of the ride turned as well. I remembered it as great fun.

"Let's do this one," I said. "I did this as a kid."

"I'll go with Dad," Emilia said.

"I'll go with Mom," Ivy agreed.

We buckled into our seats, and five seconds into the ride, I knew I'd made a terrible mistake. It wasn't the ride of my youth. Not at all. The ride of my youth moved around and back and forth but not up and down. Ivy giggled as we went around in a big circle but also ascended into the air and descended again.

"Oh my god I hate this," I said. "Oh god oh god oh god."

"Gosh," Ivy corrected me. "It's fun, Mom!"

"How long is this going to go on for? Oh Jesus, make it stop."

"Whee!" Ivy threw her arms in the air.

"This is a stupid, stupid way to die."

"I love this!"

"It's too high. Too fast."

For the rest of the day, Mike was plagued by an unshakable headache, while I kept silently repeating the phrase "Never again."

"You know," Mike said, "another way to escape the heat would be to go to a movie theater."

"You do realize we're not in America."

"Yeah, but I really want to see the new *Star Wars* movie," he said.

"Well, that's probably going to have to wait until we're back in the States."

"I don't know."

"Mike, any movie you find is going to be dubbed in Portuguese. Besides, I don't know that taking the kids to see a *Star Wars* movie in the theater is a good idea."

Sure enough, Mike proved me wrong by finding a showing of *Star Wars* without dubbing, instead using Portuguese subtitles.

"Is Dark Vader the bad guy in this one?" Emilia asked as we entered the theater.

"I haven't seen this one," I said. "I have no idea what it's about."

"Let's sit here," she said, pointing to an empty row of seats.

"We can't. We have to find our assigned seats," Mike informed her.

"Assigned seats at a movie! That's the craziest thing I've ever heard in my whole life," Emilia said.

"I hope they use life savers in this one," Ivy said. And suddenly I had an image of Darth Vader and Han Solo standing toe to toe, battling by throwing little Life Saver candies at one another.

My apprehensions of the movie were well founded. When the movie hit its climax with the death of a longtime *Star Wars* hero, Emilia began bawling beside me. "It's okay," I whispered to her in the dark theater. "It's not real. It's just a movie."

"I know," she cried, and continued to choke on her sobs. I cuddled her to my side, then looked over, expecting to see Mike doing the same with Ivy. Like her sister, Ivy was bawling, distraught at what had just taken place on the screen in front of her. Mike, however, was oblivious and sat fully engrossed in the movie.

"Mike," I whisper-shouted. No response. "Mike!" He turned to look at me. "Comfort your daughter!" I scolded.

He looked down at Ivy and realized that he'd slacked in the fatherhood department. Such is the power of the Force.

As we left the movie theater, Emilia declared that she never wanted to see the movie again. By the time we reached our temporary home, she announced that she couldn't wait to see the movie again.

"I mean, it's sad," she conceded, "but I think I'm okay now."

* * *

Avenue of Realized Dreams

A tree house, a free house,
A secret you and me house . . .

—Shel Silverstein

"Ricardo." He extended his hand for a shake. "It's very nice to meet you." Ricardo was a friend of our exchange partners and the owner of a tree house, to which we'd been invited for a one-night stay. It was located in Porecatu, about an hour away from Londrina. "I think you guys are going to have a really good time there," he said in flawless English. "Just bring a cooler with whatever you want. I'll be there when you arrive, show you around a bit, and then hand over the key. You can return it to me when you come back to Londrina. Sound good?"

"That sounds great," said Mike. "Thank you so much."

As Ricardo detailed directions to Mike, I wondered how much "showing around" could be done in regards to a tree house. What could be involved beyond a ladder and an elevated shelter? How complex could it possibly be?

After packing up and getting on the road, we noticed at the fringes of town a series of no-tell motels, known in other parts of the world as "love hotels" but in Brazil as simply motels. They cater specifically to amorous couples in need of added discretion, typically because their trysts do not involve their husbands and wives. It was impossible to drive by them and not think of the word "cooties."

When we reached the tree house, I had to reconcile the monstrosity before me with the image I'd had in my head of what a tree house actually is. I've been on the roof of my own home before, and it usually makes me a bit queasy, as heights are not my strong suit. What loomed before me was a hexagonal wooden palace sixty feet in the sky.

We climbed an intricate series of stairs and ladders that moved around the healthy limbs and incorporated them into the structure without harming the tree. I realized that Ricardo was not someone who tinkered in his spare time, and we would soon learn that he was renowned in the world of tree houses. We think of tree houses as kids' playrooms up short ladders in the backyard. This was, instead, an actual house in a tree, and Ricardo's business was aptly named Casa na Árvore, or House in a Tree. The tree house we were at was Ricardo's family's private getaway. I understood what a privilege it was for us to stay there.

While the girls and I perused the living space of the tree house, which included two sets of bunk beds, a master bedroom with a queen-sized sleeping mattress, and a living room area and kitchenette, Mike followed Ricardo back to the main gate of the property so that he might lock up for the night. As soon as they piled into their trucks and began driving away, I heard the unsettling sound of rushing water. "Girls, stay here," I said, referring to the bunk bed and living room area of the tree house. "I'll be right back." I exited the main structure to a deck-like platform with a built-in desk area and a hammock overlooking a dense jungle and shallow river. I saw water running in thick rivers down the base of the tree. There was a hose snaking along the trunk as well, and I spied a valve and contemplated turning it off but decided against it in light of the fact that I had not a clue what the hell I was doing. The tree house, despite its lofty perch, had both running water and electricity. I went to the eagle's nest, the loftiest of the tree house platforms, despite the fact that there couldn't have been anything I'd have rather done less at that moment. By crawling on to the roof of the main structure, I got a view of the water tank that supplied running water to the living quarters. It was overflowing, resulting in water raining down from the roof as well as the rivulets running along the main tree trunk. I again considered turning the valve I'd spotted further below but imagined this resulting in bursting pipes or other such calamity. If I took action, I'd likely destroy this magnificent tree house, Ricardo's life's work. If I didn't take action, I imagined a similar fate. So I did the most logical thing I could think of. I stared hard at the driveway, willing Mike to return so that I might not be the lone adult in the situation.

"As soon as you left, water starting pouring down," I said frantically, out of breath from both stress and exertion as soon as Mike returned. "The tank at the top is overflowing, and I don't know what to do!"

"Oh," Mike replied casually. "I know what to do. He said that would happen. It just means it's full, and I turn the hose off at the bottom."

"You know, you might have told me that before you left."

Once I recovered from the situation, I was able to relax and enjoy the enchantment of the place. At the base of the tree was a balance beam and slide. Two firemen's poles came down from the tree house, one smaller and intended for children, the other much higher and only for adults. I used the kiddie pole. Large swinging nests, circular couches enclosed in wicker, hung from other nearby trees. And of course we all made our way back up to the eagle's nest to enjoy the spectacular view. Mike reveled in the surrounding jungle and the fact that there was no one for miles around, while I contemplated if there really was no one for miles around, or if roving bandits waited in the forest to attack us at any moment. If there were no bandits, and there truly was no one around, I pictured snakes and big cats lying in wait. These thoughts were interrupted by a rustling noise.

"What was that? Did you guys hear that?" I asked.

"I think it came from over there." Emilia pointed to an area of dense foliage on the ground below.

"Whatever it is, it's big," said Ivy as we watched leaves move.

"Is it a jungle cat or a giant anaconda?" I asked. "Both can climb trees."

Mike elbowed me in reprimand for alarming the kids. The rustling continued for a moment until a cow lumbered out from the brush. Emilia, Ivy, and Mike all looked at me with smirks on their faces.

"Oh," I said.

Touring the rest of the property revealed it to be an estate, with extensive living quarters for farm and ranch hands, though deserted at the time of our stay, save for a few cows. We spent the afternoon at the estate's clubhouse, which included a game room, fully stocked bar, and small swimming pool. While we used both the game room and swimming pool, I'm proud to report that we showed excellent restraint when it came to the fully stocked bar.

In the evening, we returned to the tree house, and as night began to fall, Mike said, "I think I'll go turn off all the outside lights." But as soon as he did so, the inside lights of the tree house became the only lights in existence for miles around. Every bug within ten square miles descended upon us. They wiggled their way in through crevices and blanketed us in swarms when Mike opened the door to come inside. I sank, horrified, back into the darkness of the bunk beds with the children, who were entirely unfazed.

"Hmm, this is unfortunate," Mike said.

"This is the stuff of nightmares."

"Oh, it's not that big of a deal," he said, though I could barely see him through the fog of a thousand insects as he stood in the kitchen. "Let me get you another glass of wine."

"Just bring me the bottle."

The girls slept fine that night. Mike and I retreated to the master, a small private room with a queen bed. Bugs didn't permeate the room to the extent they had the kitchen and main living area, but they were still present, and after a minute or two of stillness, I'd begin scratching or frantically throw back the sheets, sure that a horde of insects was attacking.

"Honey, there's nothing there," Mike said. "Try to get some sleep."

"There *is* something there," I said. "There's *always* something there. Look, here's another." I held up a tiny speck as evidence, though in truth I'm not sure if it was a bug or an innocuous crumb of dirt.

"Just try and get some sleep," he repeated.

"What's that?"

"What's what?"

"That noise."

He listened, and I knew from his expression that I wasn't imagining it. "Oh, there's a family of little bats living in the roof of this room. Ricardo told me about them. It's nothing to worry about."

After my panic at the bugs, one might expect me to fully freak out at the mention of a family of bats, but I actually find them endearing. However, their squeaking and chattering throughout the night was yet another impediment to sleep. And then the rains began and the wind picked up. The tree began to sway. I felt queasy at the thought of how high in the air we were. What if lightning struck and we crashed to the ground? What if lightning struck and Mike and I crashed to the ground while the girls remained sixty feet in the air, cold and shivering in a half shell of a tree house, with no way to get down and no one to call for help? I turned to look at Mike, but he was fast asleep.

In the morning, we surveyed the kitchen, where every inch of space was covered in bugs, most dead, some still squirming. I used a roll of paper towels to wipe them from every surface, to leave the space in the deceptively appealing condition in which we'd found it. I looked forward to leaving. As we packed, Mike said, "This is the coolest place ever. This is my favorite part of this whole trip."

* * *

Nutritional Value

He was a bold man that first ate an oyster.

—Jonathan Swift

When the time came for us to leave Londrina, we stopped at our neighborhood bakery to say goodbye to the imposing security guard who sat perched on a stool at the café entrance during business hours. He'd learned to recognize our girls and smiled like a child himself every time he saw them. I never attributed his presence to a rash of crime but to the general custom of having security present at almost all places of business, even the most innocuous ones like a neighborhood bakery.

We took the short flight to São Paulo, a jaunt we'd become exceedingly familiar with over the previous two months, having traveled the stretch between the two cities four times in total. We arrived and took a taxi to an apartment Mike had booked on Airbnb. It was a two-bedroom, one-bathroom apartment on the seventh floor in a gated apartment complex. Although I'm not sure how many *un*gated apartment complexes there are in the city. As with any major city, crime is an ongoing concern, and São Paulo was certainly no exception.

When we showed up at the gate, we were let through by the guards after giving Mike's name, then made our way to the apartment where our host and his friend stood waiting to hand over the key. He looked like an effeminate gangster, which I've come to associate with big cities. His friend, perhaps boyfriend, was similar. He was exceptionally nice and used his phone to convey information, explaining in Portuguese that he spoke no English. He'd gone an extra step to leave us with snacks, soft drinks, and bottled water, which was much appreciated in light of the fact that we'd come straight from the airport with a mountain of luggage and no chance to purchase anything. The tiny kitchen made me think of it as "very European," which is a fancy way of saying "small" and has nothing to do with Europe. Our host seemed hesitant to leave us, which I took as a combination of apprehension over turning his home over to strangers, mixed with the fear that we were green and naïve and would likely meet an unfortunate fate during our time in São Paulo. This fear was confirmed in others we met. While checking out the facilities at the apartment complex, we met two American men on bicycles who were in the city for a few months of work.

"Do you guys need help?" one of them asked in English.

"We're fine," I answered, "just checking things out. Are you American?"

"Yes," the second one answered. "We're from Michigan."

"Any advice for spending time in São Paulo?" Mike asked.

"Be careful," the first one said gravely. "Be very careful." They looked at Emilia and Ivy.

"Yes," the other agreed. "This is not a good part of town."

"We'll be fine," I assured them, or assured myself. "We've been traveling around Brazil for two months now."

That night, we found a small restaurant and ordered beer, sodas, and fries, not the healthiest of combinations but one that would make everyone happy.

"Excuse me," I said to the waiter in Portuguese. "What are they having?" I pointed to another table where locals hovered around a platter piled high with something. It seemed like a good idea to order what the locals were eating instead of limiting ourselves to fries.

"Chicken," he said. "Do you want that?"

"Yes," I confirmed. "And a caipirinha, please. We'll also have the broccoli in garlic and olive oil." As soon as I'd seen broccoli on the menu, I got excited. The waiter returned a few minutes later with the chicken and the news that they were out of broccoli. The fried chicken looked to be a plate of chicken spines that had been fried half a dozen times. It was the least desirable part of the chicken, unless you consider a plate of chicken feet or chicken beaks a possibility, and I wasn't sure what we were supposed to do with them.

On the way back to the apartment that night, mildly drunk on caipirinhas, we stopped at a small market to let the girls pick out a treat, and also added to our basket a few packets of ramen and some microwave popcorn, foods with no nutritional value but which could be cooked in even the tiniest and most unfamiliar of kitchens. At the checkout counter, I attempted to pay and gave the clerk one hundred reals instead of ten, though I clearly had smaller bills in hand. The clerk gave me a look that told me she thought I was a stupid, rich bitch. *I'm not a stupid, rich bitch*, I wanted to say, *just a little bit drunk*.

The next day, we ventured out to the streets where endless rows of vendors hawked all manner of items, including toys, shoes, dresses, water, phone accessories, and hair clips.

"Can we walk where it's not so crowded?" I asked. The number of people milling about made it difficult for our family of four to stick together. Mike and I held tight to the girls' hands. In response to my request, Mike led us away from the crowd.

"Mom, it smells like pee," Ivy said.

"She's right," Mike agreed.

Not far ahead of us, I spied a man peeing against the wall. We realized that there was a reason the street on which we walked wasn't as crowded as the others. It was also a public toilet.

Inside the municipal market, where we enjoyed the shade and it smelled far less of urine, we found a conglomeration of vendors selling fish, lobster, eel, crab, shrimp, pig legs, halves of animals, chicken feet, cheeses, fruits, and confections. The architecture of the building was as much of an attraction as the goods for sale and included a series of striking stained-glass murals. An upper level was home to restaurants, and we decided to stop for lunch.

"Where do you want to sit?" Mike asked.

"Any of these are fine," I said.

"Well, we should definitely go to *that* restaurant," he said.

"You mean the only one that looks like it doesn't have any tables available?"

"Yes."

"Why not go to one of these that's less crowded?"

"I want to go to the restaurant that has the food that brings people back. Obviously there's going to be a reason why that one is so crowded."

"Okay, I see your point."

The long platform had railings to separate the seating of one restaurant from the next, and we made our way to the only section completely buzzing with activity, while the other restaurants waited on sparse handfuls of customers.

"I think I'm going to get one of these big meaty sandwiches," Mike said, indicating a picture on the menu of a traditional Brazilian sandwich of roast beef, called a *bauru*.

"I'll get the *bacalhau*. It says they're famous for the *bacalhau*."

"What is it?"

"Some type of fish, I think. Cod maybe." I pointed at the menu to a picture of a large, fried cylinder, like an oversized fish stick.

"What do we get?" Emilia asked.

"We can all share everything," I said. "I'll order a shrimp pastel, too. And look, you can get strawberry and orange juice. Let's try that."

The shrimp pastel, a rectangular pastry ostensibly filled with some sort of shrimp mixture, never arrived. The *bacalhau* was fishier than fish dishes should be, and I determined that yes, it might be famous, but if so, for all the wrong reasons.

"How's your sandwich?" I asked Mike. "It looks awesome."

"Have a bite," he said, passing it to me. I did so. "The meat's a little . . . questionable."

"You might have told me the meat is questionable *before* offering me a bite and handing me the sandwich."

"But then you might not have tried it," he explained.

"Thanks for that. Want to try some of my giant, creepy, fishy fish stick?"

"I'm good."

"Mom, I'm hungry," Ivy said.

"Want another bite of the sandwich?" Mike asked. She ignored him.

"I know you're hungry, sweetie. We all are." To salvage the meal, I ordered the girls a dessert pastel. It was a large pastry filled with bananas and sweetened condensed milk, topped off with vanilla ice cream and chocolate sauce. After that, there were no further complaints. We've done this often, used sweets as a means of smoothing out a situation that isn't going well, and we're fully aware that it's not creating the best and most healthful of habits in our children. It seems to teach them that when the going gets tough, sugar will make everything better. Food is love, comfort, and employed in times of stress.

We decided the restaurant was great for drinks and desserts. The strawberry and orange juice was delicious, and the restaurant had a policy of bringing a full beer to any adult who didn't have one. They would set it down in front of you without asking and add a hash mark on a small slip of paper to keep track of how many you'd been served. Until you firmly said no, you would continue to have beer placed in front of you.

After lunch, we went back downstairs to browse sections of the market we hadn't yet seen. We walked past a fruit vendor who held out samples of his produce. I told him in Portuguese that I don't speak Portuguese, thinking that might get us out of a hard sales pitch, but he was far more capable at his job than I was of evading salesmen, and he immediately switched to perfect English and began offering our family of four cut sections of pear, cherries, dragon fruit, halved strawberries nestled inside dates, and half a dozen other fruits I couldn't identify. We bought dates, strawberries, cherries, and dragon fruit, and Mike wandered ahead with the girls while I paid.

The total came to the equivalent of forty dollars. I was aghast that we somehow had been swindled so expertly. Did the fruit come packaged in a Holy Grail to justify such a price? Instead of balking or backing out of the purchase, I recognized the tourist trap and stepped in anyway. I handed over my credit card. As soon as we returned to the apartment, I removed the stickers they'd placed on the trays of fruit, indicating the price, so that Mike wouldn't see. I justified this with all of the things we'd purchased in Brazil that cost a fraction of what we were used to. I just wanted to let this one instance go. And the cherries were lovely.

* * *

The key for our apartment was on a keychain with a cross. I inspected it closely and saw that Jesus was on the cross but also that the keychain doubled as a whistle. "Hey, look," I said to Mike. "It's a whistle. So, you know, when you're in trouble, you just blow Jesus."

"You had to go there, didn't you?"

"Mom, what can we do?" Emilia asked.

"Why don't I see if I can get the key for the game room?" I offered. We'd spied a Ping-Pong table and thought it might be a game we could survive without anyone ending up in tears. I went to the guard, held up my key, and said, "*Salão de jogos?*" I knew that I needed to turn in my apartment key as collateral for the game room key. The guard smiled, spoke rapidly in Portuguese I couldn't decipher, took my key, and traded it for another one. The one he gave me had a keychain with an unfamiliar word on it. I took it back to the game room, but it didn't work. I returned to the security guard, who, I understood through my limited Portuguese and supplemental sign language, informed me that I just needed a strong man to open it for me. I knew of course that I needed no such thing. I tried the key again, with greater force and a fear that I might break the key and the lock altogether, while Mike waited with the girls nearby. Reluctantly, I asked Mike if he wanted to give it a try, but it was no use, and we were pretty sure it was the wrong key. I went back to the guard station. Two Brazilian boys, maybe ten or twelve, were hanging around. They looked at me, looked at the key, and shook their heads before turning to the guard and repeating to him in Portuguese that I wanted the key for the game room. He shuffled around for a few minutes but kept bringing back the same useless key. Then one of the boys, with a huff of exasperation, entered the security guard station, and for a moment I was afraid he would be tazed or shot on my behalf. But he emerged a second later and handed me a key, on the keychain of which were clearly the words *salão de jogos*. This was the game room key. I thanked the boys, who looked in the direction of the security guard and shook their heads, and I realized that the security guard was illiterate. I thought of Sammy, our fantastic guide in the jungle, also illiterate, and wondered what it would be like to go through life as such.

* * *

Carnival

There is no point to samba if it doesn't make you smile.

—Alma Guillermoprieto

"*Sambódromo, por favor?*"

The cab driver craned his neck to look at us in the back. "*Sambódromo?*" I repeated. I knew I'd pronounced the word correctly. How could a cab driver in São Paulo possibly not know where the *Sambódromo* was? I had to remind myself that São Paulo was a massive city and that many Brazilians ignore Carnival, just as I've been known to ignore great festivals and events in my hometown. The thinking that all Brazilians participate in Carnival is like saying all Americans participate in Mardi Gras, and our cabbie confirmed this with a confused look that seemed to say, "Oh, is that going on now?"

Our exchange partners had confessed that they make a point of staying away from big cities during Carnival, and seemed alarmed not only that we would go to São Paulo during festival time but that we'd also subject our kids to such debauchery. We were undeterred and spent two days in Londrina trying to procure tickets for one night of festivities at the *Sambódromo*. We failed to complete an online purchase and enlisted the help of Silvana, the neighbor who'd first picked us up at the airport. She called a ticketing office on our behalf but reported that it was too close to Carnival and tickets henceforth had to be purchased in person in São Paulo. We thanked her for the attempt, and she offered us a great many blessings, likely deducing that anyone who would take their kids to Carnival surely needed them. Still undeterred, Mike returned to the computer and eventually booked tickets through an agency that promised to deliver them to our location in São Paulo. It had been a tricky operation, and we were taken off guard to find that it all worked out, having half-expected to be scammed out of a small chunk of money. But the tickets were delivered as promised, and I reminded myself that nearly everyone we'd encountered in Brazil had been generous, kind, and honest to the core.

The cab driver spent a minute punching information into his phone while Mike brought up a map on his own phone. The two conferred, with much pointing and nodding, and we were on our way.

The girls had napped for a few hours that afternoon, and we'd woken them in time to prepare for our 10 p.m. departure from our apartment, which was well past their typical bedtime. I wasn't sure how one should typically dress for Carnival. On one hand, the spirit of celebration made you want to dress up, but on the other hand, would we find ourselves in a crowd of sweaty bodies with beer raining down upon us? And why exactly were we taking our kids to such a thing?

When the cab neared the giant *Sambódromo*, we found ourselves on roads choked with cars, moving with the gait of a charging snail. The giant arena was right in front of us, so we exited the cab where we were, instead of having the driver continue inching in a direction we didn't even know was correct. Exiting the vehicle at the point we did also allowed the cabbie to do a U-turn and escape the congestion before continuing in a direction that offered no such avenue of retreat.

"Hold hands, girls," I said as we walked quickly in the direction of the massive arena. We didn't see a clear main entrance but a series of smaller entrances, dependent on where your tickets were for inside the arena. We began walking, and I sensed a wary excitement from the girls at being up after dark and outside an impending big event in a foreign country. "I don't think we're in the right spot," I said to Mike. We crossed huge parking lots where thousands of performers gathered in sprawled groups, each of which was clearly delineated by their matching costumes. We saw giant hoop skirts, feathered wings, drummers, bright orange hats, and headdresses. One group wore futuristic garb, while the next appeared to be an homage to times gone by. "Seriously, Mike. I don't think we're supposed to be here. I'm pretty sure we're not supposed to be walking through the staging area before the parade."

"Just go with it," he said, charging forth. "Think of it as a bonus, like backstage passes."

"Mom, I think it's starting to rain," said Emilia.

"That's okay. A little rain won't hurt us."

We had an umbrella, but the light rain wasn't yet enough to merit its use. An umbrella was also an unwieldy option to open while navigating through crowds and thousands of people all migrating in different directions. At one point, Mike stopped to talk to a vendor, from whom he purchased a few clear ponchos.

It was a solid thirty minutes of walking before we came to our entrance, and I realized the enormity of the *Sambódromo* and feared for my children's longevity. It was enough to ask them to endure a middle-of-the-night parade. Asking them to speed walk for half an hour before the parade even started felt like pushing it.

When we finally reached the correct entrance for our designated seats, there was no line, which surprised me, given the scope of the operation. We produced our tickets, got wristbands, had our bags searched, and were let inside to an area of restrooms on one side, and food and drink vendors on the other. Passing through this area, we entered the actual *Sambódromo*. We were on the lowest level, on the same plane as the performers, having sprung to reserve an actual table, as opposed to the bleacher seats above us. A round table and four chairs were permanently affixed to the ground. In between our ground-level table and the bleacher seats were the cream of the crop in terms of seating, the equivalent of skyboxes, stocked with beer and soft drinks, with chairs and private bathrooms, and a roof to protect from rain. I wondered what they cost.

Our table with four chairs afforded us a designated area without worry of being crammed up against strangers. However, the open design of the *Sambódromo* permitted the light rain to collect on our chairs, and we used our programs to scoop as much moisture as we could from the seats before sitting down. Had we known, we would have brought towels, which we always found ourselves needing in Brazil but never seemed to have.

We settled in and purchased beer and soft drinks and skewers of beef and chicken to keep everyone happy while we waited for the parade to begin. When it did, I realized that we were not seeing a parade but an intensely intricate and choreographed performance of incomprehensible scale. We were at the end of the *Sambódromo*, which was a long avenue down which the performers marched, danced, shuffled, and pushed monstrous colorful floats.

There were seven samba schools competing that night, and each took roughly an hour to move through the length of the stadium, with fifteen-minute intermissions, totaling an eight-and-a-half-hour event. Because we were at the far end of the stadium, we could hear the roar of the crowd and the beat of the drums long before we saw the floats and dancers, which lent well to the building of anticipation as the procession reached us. But this was more than simply fantastical floats and beautiful people. Each school operates with people in very specific roles and follows an allegorical theme. There's the *Mestre-Sala* (Master of the Room, male) and *Porta-Bandeira* (Flag Bearer, female), followed by scores of dancers, floats, the *bateria* (drum section), and others in specific roles like the Queen of Drums, the Godmother of Drums, and the Carnival Muse. Each school had an overall theme, and they were scored by judges on how well the music and floats communicated that theme, as well as on rules specific to the samba school performances.

The floats and dancers of the first school told stories of slavery, brutality, revolution, war, and colonialism. And I realized then, with no small measure of relief, that Carnival can be as much about art and social commentary as it is about nearly naked women shaking their stuff. The scantily clad, in fact, were the minority in a highly diverse population of parade participants. From children to the elderly, including one woman in a wheelchair, the performers had all body types and included more than a few women who hadn't been born as such. It was all-inclusive, even featuring a group of special-needs children.

The troupes representing each school danced and sang to the same song for their particular school for the hour they made their way the length of the *Sambódromo*, and the logistics of the operation were as impressive as the performances. Behind each mammoth float, we'd spy a group of men pushing the float, sweating and singing as they did so. Along the sides of the lane, in between the spectators and performers, designated people encouraged the performers and helped them keep time, stay on pace, and follow their strict choreography. The experience for the performers seemed was different depending on if you were on the ground or on a float. While scantily clad beauties smiled, waved, and shook their hips from perches high on the moving floats, a man in his sixties shuffled by on the ground, trying to keep up with the moves of his group, but he looked tired and as if about to have a heart attack. A woman of about the same age made eye contact with me, and we had an unspoken exchange in which she told me she was exhausted, and I replied that I understood but she was almost at the end and doing great. It seemed a long time to dance in heavy costume, for even the most fit humans. More than a few performers wore expressions of "What the hell did I get myself into?"

The floats were as varied as the costumes, and the sheer scope of them was hard to comprehend. I could only wonder at the amount of money and time that went into constructing massive tigers, buildings, Neptune, jungles, all on wheels and with the capacity to showcase hundreds of dancers. There were tributes to indigenous tribes and an entire school whose theme revolved around France. One group centered on music, with performers in costumes that had bell-bottoms, disco balls on their heads, giant fake trumpets attached to their capes behind them, and giant fake guitars attached to their costumes in the front. There were deep-sea costumes and cavemen. A security guard meandered around and smiled at me when I made eye contact. I smiled back and studied his boyish face and oversized uniform, wondering if he could be more than fifteen years old.

At the end of each samba school parade came the muse. This is the woman in spiked heels, giant feathered headdress, and not much else, the woman who the cameras come out for and who we picture when we think of Carnival. Bronzed bodies, impossibly round and elevated breasts, and the ability to shake their buttocks as if each cheek was an appendage. The physical feats that these women were capable of were more than impressive, and I'm not just referring to the aforementioned shaking of buttocks. Maybe I was so impressed because I can't even walk in such heels, much less dance. And even in shoes in which I am comfortable and grounded, my dancing is painfully awkward, even my attempts at a casual swaying of the hips.

Between each samba school's hour-long parade, there was a brief intermission, during which an ambulance traveled the length of the *Sambódromo*, just to make sure the exhausted performers, the ones who'd looked like they might collapse when they passed by, hadn't actually done so. The ambulance was followed by a street sweeper and an additional fifteen minutes of intermission while the next samba school readied for their big moment. As the muse exited the *Sambódromo* (to a great many people's disappointment), I grabbed both Emilia and Ivy by the hands and said, "Girls, let's run to the bathroom!" It had occurred to me, a second too late, that if we waited for intermission to use the bathroom, we'd likely wait in line for half an hour.

"Why do we have to run?" Ivy panted.

"I don't have to go!" Emilia protested.

"Just trust me."

In line, not too far from the front, justifying the sudden sprint, I explained it to them.

"But, Mom, I don't have to go," Emilia repeated.

When we finally made it into a bathroom stall, to find a toilet with no seat, I instructed Emilia just to hover over it.

"Okay," she said, then promptly sat down on the seat-less rim of the toilet and began an extensive urination, contrary to her previous assertions of not having to go.

We returned to our table to watch Pantene ads flash on huge screens above the bleacher seats, and hundreds of dancers progress through the *Sambódromo*. As amazing as it was, at some point you have to ask yourself, how many hours of a spectacular parade can you actually watch?

As dawn approached, I walked over to Mike and broached the subject of leaving. There was still an entire samba school coming, but I felt we'd had a largely positive experience and shouldn't push our luck. We left the *Sambódromo* at 6 a.m. and found a cab to return us to our apartment.

As we entered the apartment and readied ourselves to go to sleep at six thirty in the morning, Mike said, "Girls, I just want to let you know how proud I am of you."

"Yes," I agreed. "You girls did awesome."

"What did we do?" Ivy asked in confusion.

"Not every kid could stay up all night and be so well behaved," Mike explained.

"Well, thanks for letting us go to the parade," Emilia said.

We tucked them in and, as we crawled into bed ourselves, talked about our daughters' adaptability not only on that night but also for the midnight celebration of Christmas in the Amazon and the New Year's Eve party on Copacabana Beach.

"You'd think there'd be at least one tantrum in there," Mike said.

"Maybe we're beyond that stage," I said hopefully.

"Or just maybe," Mike ventured, "our children are better travelers than we are."

* * *

Tchau Tchau

São Paulo is the third-largest Italian city in the world outside Italy,
the largest Japanese city outside Japan, the biggest Portuguese city
outside Portugal, the major Spanish city outside Spain,
and the third largest Lebanese city outside Lebanon . . .

—*Insight Guides: Brazil*

São Paulo is a massive city, one that is said to have more people of Italian descent than Rome itself. As such, and as enthusiastic consumers of Italian wine and food, it was entirely appropriate that we spend some of our few remaining days seeking out Bixiga, São Paulo's version of Little Italy.

We left the apartment and headed for the metro station. To do this, we had to pass what I came to think of as Wedding Row. Our apartment was certainly in a dodgy area of town, where the one not-so-scary group of buildings housed stores with wedding dresses.

"When I get married, I want that one," Ivy said, pointing to an elegant white dress with a long train. "Or maybe that one," she corrected, pointing to a ridiculously poufy gown that made me think of the Stay Puft Marshmallow Man from the 1984 *Ghostbusters* movie.

"I don't know if I want to get married," Emilia said.

"You don't have to," Mike and I responded in unison.

"Oh no, wait! I totally want to get married, because I want to wear *that* dress," she said, pointing to a blizzard of satin and pearls.

"Please don't ever get married just so you can wear a dress," I said.

"Don't worry, honey," Mike assured me. "She's eight years old."

In Bixaga, we discovered a restaurant called Roperto, which I don't know how to describe other than to say it felt like home, because if I had a family crest, it would somehow incorporate the elements of wine and pasta. The experience was enjoyable for everyone, so much so that we would return two more times before the end of the trip.

For other meals, we explored the small, cheap street cafés, which exist with as much frequency as Starbucks in the United States.

"They have an omelet," I said as we sat at one such café for breakfast. "And then they have a 'complete omelet.'"

"Well, why don't we get one of each," Mike suggested. "Maybe the kids will eat the plain omelet."

"I wonder what the complete one will be. Maybe it will have tomatoes and a bunch of veggies cooked in there."

The plain omelet turned out to be a ham and cheese omelet, while the complete omelet (or full omelet) was a ham and cheese omelet laying like a thick cheesy, protein blanket on top of mounds of white rice and french fries and served with a side of beans.

"It's kind of silly for breakfast, don't you think? I mean, rice and fries and beans, it just seems like a ridiculous amount of carbs," I said.

"Well, until you think about the fact that in the States we eat our eggs with hash browns and home fries and toast."

"You have a point."

"Mom," Ivy said as she picked at the fries. "What's that man doing?"

I looked up to see a homeless man headed our way with outstretched palms. As he reached our table, one of the café employees intercepted him and shooed him away.

"I think he was going to ask us for money," I explained.

"What's he doing now?" Emilia asked.

We watched as the man rooted through a trash can outside, then dashed back into the café and swiftly grabbed a mayonnaise packet from a condiment shelf, and returned back outside to eat someone's discarded snack.

On our walk back to the apartment, in the middle of the day, with bright sunshine and heavy heat, we saw a man dressed in suit and tie walking toward us on the sidewalk. As he neared, I noticed something on his forehead. And as we passed him, we saw that he had recently had the shit kicked out of him. He bled from cuts on his face and head and hands, and likely other places beneath his suit. He looked scared, and we knew that whatever altercation happened had taken place within the previous half hour. He spoke to us, but we held our daughters' hands tightly and walked on by. I would spend the next few hours thinking of all the things I should have done, even if only to say, "I don't speak Portuguese," as an explanation for our complete failure to help him in some way.

"I had no idea when I booked this apartment that it was in a rough side of town," Mike said.

"Well, there are many rough places in this town, and I'm sure there are plenty that are far rougher than this."

"That's true."

While we hadn't sought out the favela tours to get a closer look at life in some of Brazil's poorer neighborhoods, neither had we wanted to wall ourselves up in a hotel for tourists. Though parts of our adventure had been grittier than anticipated, the trying or uncomfortable experiences are often the dearest in hindsight.

We turned a corner and watched a parade progress up the street. Carnival was still going on, and in addition to galas and the *Sambódromo* parade, there are *blocos*, smaller neighborhood parades that take place throughout the city. These are comprised of people drinking, dancing, and drumming. At this particular *bloco*, we had the unfortunate opportunity to witness drunk men peeing against a wall, and another drunk man pause, put his hands on his knees, and vomit a little bit before standing up and continuing along with the party.

"You know," said Mike, "I think tonight we should go to a different part of town. Maybe go somewhere sort of nice to eat, since we're running out of time on this trip."

I watched Vomit Man sway behind a small float that led revelers around the block. "Yeah," I agreed, "I'm up for that."

That evening, we had reservations at a rooftop restaurant. I put on a dress, gussied up the girls, and we set out for the metro to locate our spot for dinner. We emerged from our metro stop to find ourselves in the middle of another *bloco*. People were dressed in all manner of costume, drinking, dancing, and laughing. I looked at our attire and said to Mike, "Suddenly I feel overdressed."

"Me, too," he said.

A second later, when we located the building that was home to the rooftop restaurant, we were turned away because we were underdressed. Mike was wearing shorts. They were nice shorts, topped off with a white linen shirt, and he looked better groomed and more preppy than his usual self, but apparently not good enough for the restaurant. We existed in a fashion limbo, and no one would have us, as we were not outlandish enough to fit in with the party on the street, yet not elegant enough to be let inside to dine.

As the doorman turned us away, a waiter fresh off of his shift overheard the conversation and told us of another restaurant we might like. "It's not far, another good restaurant I really recommend," he said. "I'm happy to show you where it is." We were thankful for his time and accepted the offer. He led us to an Italian restaurant with an elegant atmosphere and waiters who enthusiastically cut Emilia and Ivy's pizza into bite-sized pieces.

There are plenty of things to do with children in São Paulo that don't involve dragging them to all-night parties or exposing them to drunk people, and we decided to explore what some of those options were. We took our daughters to a one-hour play of *The Lion King*, intended for an audience of children. And though they couldn't understand Portuguese, they knew the story well enough to follow along. It was a wonderful production, though for musical numbers, the actors adopted an odd theatrical practice of lip-syncing to the songs played through the sound system, instead of singing themselves, before going back to speaking their lines when the songs were over.

The São Paulo Zoo could not have been more disappointing, as much for the filth as because of the attendees. It was perfectly acceptable for people to taunt and harass the animals. Entire herds of children would chant in unison for big cats to emerge, for monkeys to entertain, and for otherwise nocturnal beings to wake up and dance a jig.

By contrast, the São Paulo Aquarium was phenomenal. We first learned that there are different words for "shark," depending on whether you are more likely to eat the shark or if the shark is more likely to eat you. Fat, yellow eels glowed in dim aquariums. We walked through the replicas of airport terminals, emerging into Africa, Indonesia, and Australia, where we'd find wildlife native to that particular continent. Exhibits weren't limited to aquatic life, and we observed lazing kangaroos, a wombat dining on roughage, a meerkat enclosure far more impressive than the one the zoo kept, and bats the size of toddlers.

"They definitely make the most of their gift shops," Mike noted, as souvenirs could be purchased not at one main shop but throughout the aquarium, for sale in between various exhibits. We moved on to seals and sea lions and a lone, still manatee.

"This exhibit seems sad," I said. "I'm impressed with all of the others, but I don't know about this one. Is it even alive? Aren't manatees social creatures?"

"Maybe it's just sleeping," said Mike. "For the most part, everything here looks really well cared for."

"Definitely better than the zoo," I agreed.

"Look, Mom! Polar bears!" Ivy pointed to the star exhibit ahead of us.

"Just wait, Ivy," instructed Mike. "We'll get there in a minute. Don't run ahead." A polar bear then stood, walked to the edge of a giant pool, and jumped in. "Yes!" said Mike, at which point he jumped the railing, abandoned his family, and ran ahead.

The bear got out a moment later and went back to a more sedentary state.

"Aw, I wish we could see that again," said Emilia.

"I think this is the last exhibit, so let's follow this path out," I said. The path led down a level and passed by the same polar bear exhibit, this time presenting an underwater view. We were the only spectators at the time, just as the polar bear above jumped back in the water.

"Whoa!" we all yelled. The bear swam an underwater lap, heading back up to the surface at the exact spot where we stood, three inches of barrier away from the brush of his fur. He took about twenty more laps along the same route, and we stood mesmerized not only by the bear but also by the fact that of all the places I'd thought I might one day see a polar bear up close, Brazil had never made the list.

On our final full day in Brazil, we decided to check out something called Kidzania, which had been recommended as one of the top activities to do with children in São Paulo. It was located inside a mall but appeared to occupy a massive amount of square footage. I wasn't sure what to expect, and we almost didn't enter because of the expense.

"This is like the cost of a big amusement park in the States!" I said.

"What do you think? Should we do it?" Mike said.

"Well, we're here, so I guess so." The employees at the entrance to Kidzania didn't speak English, so we weren't too sure what we were getting into. Through minimal Portuguese supplemented with sign language, we were directed to walk through a replica of an airport terminal, much like what we'd done at the aquarium. Only this time, we landed in Kidzania, a world where children can work jobs to earn money, spend that money on various forms of entertainment, *procure a Kidzania driver's license*, and other activities that mimic commerce and its corresponding responsibilities in adult life.

Emilia and Ivy took pilot lessons, worked in a surgery and in a pediatric ward, made pizzas in a restaurant, participated in a rock band, and of course procured their drivers' licenses and drove small red cars around a track. It was a fantastic experience but would have been even more so if we'd fully grasped the concept from the start. We treated it like an arcade, doling out money for them to do things, instead of putting them in charge of the money and giving them the invaluable experience of deciding what and where to spend and earn. As it was, when the Kidzania money they'd been given upon entry was exhausted, I asked where we could purchase more, and only then did I understand that you can't purchase more but must instead earn money through one of the various jobs available. In addition to the girls' chosen activities, children could deliver mail, become firefighters or policemen, work at the Kidzania newspaper, and take shifts at the Customs and Immigration office. Benches lined the "streets" of Kidzania for parents to sit on, which was necessary, as parents were not allowed inside any of the stores but instead had to wait outside like patient Labradors, though the children were in view at all times.

"That was the coolest thing ever!" Emilia asserted when it was time to go.

"Can we come back?" Ivy asked.

"We're flying back to America tomorrow," Mike explained.

"But I'm sure there are other Kidzanias," I said. "I'll look it up. Maybe we'll stumble upon another one some day."

When I found Kidzania online, I discovered that, as of yet,

there are no locations in the United States. There are franchising opportunities, though, so as soon as I have $20 million, it might be something I'll pursue.

* * *

Sleep was elusive that night. The apartment was stifling, and I had the unfortunate feeling of bugs crawling over my skin. And if I did have bugs crawling on my skin, I didn't want it to be on my last night in Brazil, because what if they were bed bugs and I transported them back to the United States and infested our home in Boise? But then I thought of the homeless camps our cab had passed earlier that evening, with people sprawled on the ground on pieced-together platforms made from found items. I thought of the man eating from the trash and swiping a mayonnaise packet to accompany his find. Bed bugs (which were only in my mind) were an entirely manageable problem.

Our cab ride to Guarulhos Airport the next day was another reminder of how lucky we are. Our driver missed the exit for GRU, missed the terminal, and missed the departure lane. I wondered if he was trying to extend our cab ride to collect a bigger fee. But when he finally delivered us to the airport and insisted we cut the fare on the meter in half, I realized that he was more likely illiterate. Probably adept at navigating between the major landmarks of the city of São Paulo, venturing outside of the city presented greater challenges in the form of unintelligible signs.

The advantages in life we've been dealt produce gratitude but didn't inspire a sense of pity for the Brazilians we'd encountered along our journey. The sense of joy present in daily Brazilian life, from the very poor to the very privileged, is a cultural blessing, one that manifested itself everywhere from the Amazonian jungle to Rio's Copacabana Beach to the hostels of the tiny coastal towns we'd visited. It was a country of smiles and rhythms of which, for a short time, we were delighted to be a part.

"Do we have lots of time at the airport or do we get right on the plane?" Emilia asked.

"Lots of time," I answered.

"What are we going to do?"

"Push-ups!" Mike declared.

"I'm not doing push-ups, Dad," Ivy said.

"Sit-ups?"

"Okay," she relented. "I'll do some sit-ups. And then maybe we can have a treat."

"Are you guys excited about going home?" I asked.

"Yeah," said Emilia. "I really like America. But Brazil was pretty cool, too. Except it's really hot here and I don't speak good Portuguese."

"Where will our next trip be?" Ivy asked.

"We'll tell you when it's a sure thing," Mike answered. "But for now I'll just give you two clues. It's not hot, and they don't speak Portuguese."

"It's Paris," Emilia asserted. "Paris or China, I bet. Wait, do they speak Portuguese there?"

"Wherever it is, I wonder what kind of treats they'll have," said Ivy.

I smiled at Mike. "Well, girls, I guess you'll just have to wait and see."

* * *

Acknowledgments

Thank you, Jim Barron. You were like a fairy godmother when I needed one. That's not weird, is it? There are many other people deserving of thanks for their encouragement and support as well. Most of them are the usual suspects. (You know who you are.) Since I didn't dedicate this book to my husband and daughters, I have to take the time to acknowledge them here. This life wouldn't be possible without their wit, energy, love, and indomitable sense of adventure.

COMING SOON . . .

Vagabonding with Kids: Alaska
Vagabonding with Kids: Mexico
Vagabonding with Kids: Spain

If you enjoyed this book,
please consider posting a review online.

Follow Vagabonding with Kids at

Facebook.com/VagabondingWithKids
Twitter.com/VagabondingKids
Pinterest.com/VagabondKids
Instagram.com/VagabondingWithKids

To find out more about the Turner family and how
they work abroad, set up home exchanges, and handle
homeschooling, download their free travel guide at
VagabondingWithKids.com.

If you have a destination to recommend or would like to
contact the Turners, e-mail amanda@akturner.com.

Epigraph Sources

Chapter 1, "Brazilian Blessings": Christopher Dawson.

Chapter 2, "Brontosaurus for Dinner": "What Do Brazilians Eat Most," *Flavors of Brazil*, August 12, 2011, accessed online August 29, 2016, http://flavorsofbrazil.blogspot.com/2011/08/what-do-brazilians-eat-most.html.

Chapter 3, "Personal Rain Cloud": Christopher Elliott, "Passenger shaming: Fair or Foul?," *USA Today*, April 11, 2016, accessed online August 29, 2016, http://www.usatoday.com/story/travel/advice/2016/04/11/passenger-shaming/82785276/.

Chapter 4, "Welcome to the Jungle": Amazon Gero Tours Manaus, accessed online August 29, 2016, http://amazongero.com/jungle-excursions/.

Chapter 5, "The Christmas Piranha": *Piranha*, directed by Scott P. Levy (Burbank: Concorde, New Horizons, 1995), accessed online August 30, 2016, http://www.imdb.com/title/tt0114137/trivia?tab=qt&ref_=tt_trv_qu.

Chapter 6, "Marco, Judy, and Other Imaginary Friends": Zsa Zsa Gabor.

Chapter 7, "Nana Loses Her Shit": Sophocles.

Chapter 8, "Every Dog Has His Apron Dress": Cesar Millan.

Chapter 9, "Christ the Reminder": "Rio de Janeiro—A City where Poverty, Indulgence, Crime, Celebration, Beauty, Passion and Future all Live in a Strange Harmony," *The Counterintuitive*, accessed online September 15, 2016, http://www.thecounterintuitive.com/destinations/south-america/brazil/rio-de-janeiro-a-city-where-poverty-indulgence-crime-celebration-beauty-passion-and-future-all-live-in-a-strange-harmony/.

Chapter 10, "Flight of the Opossum": John Steinbeck.

Chapter 11, "Lessons in Patience": Aristotle.

Chapter 12, "Guarapari": "Hot Spots: Earth's 5 Most Naturally Radioactive Places," Web Ecoist, accessed online September 16, 2016, http://webecoist.momtastic.com/2013/01/22/hot-spots-earths-5-most-naturally-radioactive-places/.

Chapter 13, "Attack of the Birthday Beetles": Bill Vaughan.

Chapter 14, "If You Like Piña Coladas": Jenna Francisco, "5 Best Street Foods in Brazil," *About Travel,* accessed online September 16, 2016, http://gobrazil.about.com/od/brazilianfooddrink/tp/5-Best-Street-Foods-in-Brazil.htm.

Chapter 15, "The Chocolate Factory": Frances O'Grady.

Chapter 16, "Capoeira Etiquette": James McAvoy.

Chapter 17, "Morning Call": Shreya Ghoshal.

Chapter 18, "Space to Breathe": Ellen Burstyn.

Chapter 19, "Playmaster": Albert Einstein.

Chapter 20, "Avenue of Realized Dreams": Shel Silverstein, "Tree House," *Where the Sidewalk Ends* (New York: HarperCollins, 1974), 79.

Chapter 21, "Nutritional Value": Jonathan Swift.

Chapter 22, "Carnival": Alma Guillermoprieto.

Chapter 23, "Tchau Tchau": *Brazil*, Insight Guides (Apa Publications, 2014), 187.